PENGUIN BOOKS

memo for a saner world

Bob Brown was born in Oberon, New South Wales and moved to Tasmania in the 1970s. He worked for many years as a medical practitioner, and was a founding member of the Wilderness Society and the Australian Bush Heritage Fund. From 1983 to 1993 he held a seat in Tasmania's House of Assembly, and in 1996 was elected to the Australian Senate. He has won many awards for his work, including the 1987 United Nations Environment Program Global 500 Award, and the 1990 Goldman Environmental Prize. In 1996 the BBC's *Wildlife* magazine named him the World's Most Inspiring Politician.

D0872868

This book is printed on paper sourced
from sustainable (plantation) forests

memo for a saner world

BOB BROWN

PENGUIN BOOKS

Penguin Books

Penguin Group (Australia)
250 Camberwell Road, Camberwell, Victoria 3124, Australia
Penguin Books Ltd
80 Strand, London WC2R 0RL, England
Penguin Group (USA) Inc.
375 Hudson Street, New York, New York 10014, USA
Penguin Books, a division of Pearson Canada
10 Alcorn Avenue, Toronto, Ontario, Canada M4V 3B2
Penguin Group (NZ)
Cnr Airborne and Rosedale Roads, Albany, Auckland, New Zealand
Penguin Books (South Africa) (Pty) Ltd
24 Sturdee Avenue, Rosebank, Johannesburg 2196, South Africa
Penguin Books India (P) Ltd
11, Community Centre, Panchsheel Park, New Delhi 110 017, India

First published by Penguin Group (Australia),
a division of Pearson Australia Group Pty Ltd, 2004

10 9 8 7 6 5 4 3 2 1

Design by Miriam Rosenbloom © Penguin Group (Australia)
Cover photography by Ted Mead
Index by Russell Brooks
Typeset in 11/16pt Sabon by Post Pre-press Group, Brisbane, Queensland
Printed and bound in Australia by McPhersons Printing Group,
Maryborough, Victoria

National Library of Australia
Cataloguing-in-Publication data:

Brown, Bob, 1944– .
  Memo for a saner world.
  Includes index.
  ISBN 0 14 300034 9.
  1. Green Party (Australia). 2. Green movement – Australia.
  3. Australia – Politics and government. I. Title.

320.580994

www.penguin.com.au

Contents

Introduction   1

Earth Spirit   5

The Franklin Blockade   17

Global Warming: A Global Warning   36

One Person, One Value   60

The Styx Valley: The Valley of the Giants   80

How Hyundai Will Decimate a
    Little Aussie Traveller   106

The Balance of Power:
    How the Greens Behave in Government   117

Antarctica: The Last Wild Continent   137

Indigenous Australia   155

The Fragile Coast: The Bay of Fires   165

Farmhouse Creek and the Role of the Law   176

Guns and Gelignite:
    Violence Towards Greens   187

Tiger Economies: Costing the Earth   203

George W. Bush in Australia:
  Manners Before Human Rights   214

Natural Philanthropy:
  The Australian Bush Heritage Fund   234

APPENDIX I: A 10-Point Plan for Future
  Prime Minsters   245

APPENDIX II: Charter of the Global Greens   247

ACKNOWLEDGEMENTS   267

INDEX   270

Introduction

Australia is, per capita, the world's wealthiest country in terms of natural resources. The conventional wisdom is to cash these in so that we become the world's richest people. But how likely is that to make us any happier? In fact, the rate of clinical depression in the West has been rising since the 1950s. Richness of spirit cannot be bought across the counter.

Green wisdom, on the other hand, is to capitalise on Australia's wealth by charting an independent role in world affairs, and by so doing improve the prospects of all the world's people, safeguarding the global environment and human security. This intertwining of social equality and democracy with environmental protection is the mainstay of the Greens' footbridge to a better future.

Of course, fairness begins at home. In Australia, the policies of the Greens are directed towards cradle-to-grave public health and education, a reversal of the

1

nation's ever-worsening environmental indices, and enhanced employment and workplace conditions. We Greens rate above par in our political energy. In a period of government obsessed with the rule of the market, our advocacy has directly influenced the freeing of East Timor and the end of mandatory sentencing of Aboriginal children, helped slow the drift of funding away from public schools and medicine, and applied a strong stay on the erosion of civil liberties in the name of fear and terror.

Anyone who was surprised by my stand on the issue of refugees in the run-up to the November 2001 federal election should read the Charter of the Global Greens in the appendices of this book. In August of that year the Norwegian freighter the *Tampa*, at Australia's request, picked up more than 400 boat people who were at risk – and was then ordered by John Howard to stay out of Australian waters. After talking the matter over with Ben Oquist in the Greens Senate office, and with the Greens charter guiding every step of the way, I held an immediate press conference to defend the human rights of the refugees, as well as the humanitarian dignity of Australia. The *Tampa*, I made it clear, should be brought to Australia and its refugees treated in accordance with the law.

The result was an instant barrage of abusive mail, including bullets and pictures of nooses, and then, three months later, a doubling of the Greens' vote across the nation. The green alternative had struck a chord.

Some people worry that a vote for the Greens is a wasted vote, but in fact it has double the value. Under Australia's preferential voting system, if your minor-party candidate is not elected, your whole vote goes to your major-party preference. Better still, an increase in the Greens' vote indicates to the big parties where your real policy preference lies. Those who wonder how the Greens would handle power will be helped by the chapter 'The Balance of Power' – we Greens have already shown that we can win important gains for the community and the environment through a role in government, even during turbulent times.

This book is not a comprehensive text on Greens politics. It consists of stories from along the road I have taken, from my years as an environmental campaigner concerned for all humanity to being a Greens senator, with discussion of some of the issues on the way. For obvious reasons the book is Tasmania-centric in parts, but the issues these chapters encompass – such as the logging of native forests and the threat to coastlines – are the same elsewhere in Australia and indeed in the rest of the world.

I am acutely aware that so many of the friends I have worked with through the years – from the Franklin blockade to the foundation of the Australian Bush Heritage Fund and the Greens, and my years in elected office – aren't named between these covers. And yet every venture has been a joint one, with like-minded people and special individuals who each deserve an accolade and have my great thanks.

It is a fortunate life if, at 59, a person feels more optimistic and fulfilled than ever before. That's me. I love my job; there is constant reward in seeing people join the Greens, and, most of all, in the contribution we are making to Australia's future wellbeing. My political awareness unfolded during the Cold War, with its underpinning philosophy of mutually assured (nuclear) destruction. The alternative of a world united in sharing resources, and diverting the money spent on arms in order to eradicate child poverty, makes as much good sense now as it did then, and appeals to the finer instincts in us all.

The Greens are the world's political antidepressant. I hope this memo for a saner world will strike a chord with you too.

Bob Brown
Liffey, 2004

Earth Spirit

The Earth is the cradle of our existence. The curl on our ears was not fashioned for television, but for the need to pick up the faintest sounds from the forest floor. We are all born bonded to nature; that's why we put depictions of flowers and forests, rather than bulldozers or log piles, on our walls. Humanity's happiness, if not its entire future, is tied to its responsibility to end the rapid destruction of the Earth's living mantle.

How does modern society break the addiction that is leading to this destruction? It is hooked on goods, tantalised by shops, mesmerised by money. For its own sake, it must fast-forward to a state of reasonable balance with the Earth; we must change from being short-sighted exploiters to long-sighted guardians of the planet.

This idea is not foreign to our culture. The Western tradition has a lively history of arguing the case against excessive materialism. Hildegard of Bingen (1098–1179)

warned that the misuse of Creation would invite punishment. The Franciscan theologian St Bonaventure
(1221–74) beseeched that God be honoured 'in every
creature lest perchance the entire universe rise against
you'. That credo remains potent. The contemporary
'Green Patriarch' of Constantinople's Eastern Orthodox
Church, Bartholomew I, says, 'To commit a crime
against the natural world is a sin.' John Paul II – the current Pope – insists that for present-day Christians 'duty
towards nature and the Creator [is] an essential part of
their faith'.

The argument that Judaeo-Christian or Islamic philosophy is the root cause of the problem – because their god
issued the warrant for humans to exploit the rest of life
on Earth – has its limits. Besides giving humans domin-
ion over the Earth, these religions also invoke the duty
of custodianship. It is freewheeling materialism which
has corrupted our reverence for Creation, and which has
supplanted the idea of humans as custodians with that of
humans as unrestrained exploiters. While materialism's
ethic favours the profiteer over the custodian, the world's
religions have a huge role to play in ensuring things are
put right. As Seyyed Hossein Nasr, Professor of Islamic
Studies at George Washington University in the United
States, said in 1994, a mullah making a call in a mosque
for environmental action will have a far greater effect
than any government plea.

The fact that the Bush White House, Blair's Number 10 Downing Street, and Prime Minister Howard at Kirribilli House all lay claim to Christianity in governance does not make it so. A better test would be to ask what Christ would think of billion-dollar armaments industries existing alongside the enormous gap between rich and poor, while these politicians who have the power to stop such an evil promote it. Nevertheless all the people at the White House go to morning prayers and presumably feel quite good about themselves. President Bush should ask the very old and wise American Catholic priest Thomas Berry to lead a morning session. Berry believes that 'Our ethical traditions know how to deal with suicide, homicide and even genocide, but these traditions collapse entirely when confronted with biocide, the killing of the life systems of the earth, and geocide, the devastation of the earth itself.'

The deep connection between humans and nature is reflected in all the great world traditions, from those of the Native Americans to China's Taoists. Tibet's exiled fourteenth Dalai Lama has travelled the world and witnessed the violence of materialist politics, but calmly appeals to the dragon of the marketplace: 'Until now, you see, Mother Earth has somehow tolerated sloppy house habits. But now human use, population, and technology have reached that certain stage where Mother Earth no longer accepts our presence with silence.' The last time this warm-hearted man was in Canberra, in 2002, Prime Minister Howard refused to see him, so I hosted his reception at Parliament House – a very crowded, delightful event with guests from all the political parties.

The idea of responsibility to the Earth as our life source and spiritual anchor echoes through modern environmentalism. John Muir (1838–1914) left Scotland for the United States as an eleven-year-old and overcame daily beatings from his evangelical father to become a pioneer of the Western conservation movement. He helped create a number of national parks, including Yosemite and the Grand Canyon, but died during the failed campaign to save California's Hetch Hetchy Valley from a dam.

His anger with the dam-builders echoes down the years: 'These temple destroyers, devotees of ravaging commercialism, seem to have a perfect contempt for Nature, and, instead of lifting their eyes to the God of the Mountains, lift them to the Almighty Dollar.' President Theodore Roosevelt went walking with Muir and agreed with him on the need to keep human exploitation out of the remaining wildness: 'Leave it as it is,' he said. 'The ages have been at work on it, and man can only mar it.'

President Bush, inexperienced in both nature and solitude, is incapable of such thinking.

The 1970s saw the evolution of deep ecology, a term coined by Norwegian professor of philosophy Arne Naess.

He contrasted an approach of deep enquiry with the false certainty of shallow materialism, commenting that the real question was 'Which society, which education, which form of religion is beneficial for all life on the planet as a whole?' To which I would add, Which politics? These are powerfully pertinent questions in a world where the rich have decided to ignore a billion of their fellow human beings living in grinding, degrading poverty.

Judith Wright McKinney, Australian poet, environmentalist, and campaigner for Aboriginal power, was a driving force in setting up the Australian Conservation Foundation in the 1960s. By the 1990s she was dismayed at the way environmentalists had been co-opted by government and corporations, and at the phenomenon of greenwash. In a letter to environmental activist Milo Dunphy in 1993 she wondered, 'Do we have a genetic fault resulting in our bowing our heads to the powerful interests whatever they do? Let's at least refuse to spend more time on nonsenses . . . Reports and Analyses . . . intended to waste our time.'

She was warning campaigners to avoid the endless inquiries, committees and analyses set up by governments when issues of environmental destruction become contentious for them. There have been twenty or thirty reports into the destruction of Tasmania's forests, for example, consuming years of environmentalists' hard work and time, yet logging is now proceeding at record rates.

Never put public action second to an inquiry, particularly one presided over by a non-environmentalist. Governments and business are masterful at stacking inquiries and diverting campaigners' energies. There is no substitute for being on the streets or at the ballot boxes. The impulse to be conciliatory to the market fundamentalists needs tempering with Albert Einstein's insight: 'A problem can not be solved with the same consciousness that created it.'

Indian global activist and writer Vandana Shiva puts her finger on the central significance of spirit in world affairs: 'A spiritual leaning used to mean total inactivity in the world, while activism tended to be associated with violence. But suddenly the only people who seem to have the courage to act are the deeply spiritual – because it's only those who know there is another world, another dimension, who are not intimidated by the world of organized power.'

Vandana Shiva and I, together with Friends of the Earth's Ricardo Navarro from El Salvador, led a walk-out on the final day of the 2002 Earth Summit in Johannesburg. A sense of resigned pessimism had overcome the 35 000 people at the conference as the world powers backed a 'trust us and do nothing' outcome. The Australian officials had written instructions from the Howard government to oppose any binding outcomes for the environment. So there were no binding outcomes – not on fisheries, forests, biodiversity, global warming or global poverty.

As we walked out of the conference foyer, US Secretary of State Colin Powell was giving his much-awaited speech in the plenary hall. He was stunned into silence by interjections from the audience and jeers for the Bush administration's finger-wagging at the world. Powell looked totally nonplussed as far better informed delegates reacted to his admonition of Africa's reticence to accept genetically engineered grain shipments from the United States as drought relief. My workmate Ben Oquist, who had managed to get an entry ticket to the hall, was arrested and bundled out along with a score of other peaceful protesters.

A multinational group of campaigners had quietly occupied the adjacent cafes in a sit-in, protesting the scuttling of the Earth Summit's bid to tackle poverty and environmental destruction. These people were attacked by armed police; some were beaten up as they lay in the forecourt.

In spite of such aggressive responses, our bond with the Earth must show itself through collective peaceful pro-test and positive politics. Violence is not an alternative. As the Dalai Lama says, 'Although there is a limit to what we as individuals can do, there is no limit to what a universal response might achieve.' He added that if he were a voter, he would vote for one of the environmental parties.

Long ago I ceased to believe in religious dogma. What I do see is the continual unfolding of the human spirit, or consciousness, and an awareness greater than that in any other creature on Earth. The universe, through us, is evolving towards experiencing, understanding and making choices about its future. We are the universe thinking.

This is a fragile thing. The mind depends on the physical self, and so the unfolding of human awareness depends on the safety of human life, which in turn depends on the health of the planet. There may be other minds out there among those billions of stars like our Sun, but as far as we know now we are the lone unfurling mind of the universe. Our responsibility is much greater than for ourselves alone.

On this beautiful planet, in this astonishing universe, the drama of human survival is the ultimate issue of our time, and our impending extinction the ultimate environmental pressure. The outcome depends on whether our collective goodwill towards life on Earth can draw back into control the blinkered self-indulgence of the age.

Pope John Paul II has said, 'It is manifestly unjust that a privileged few should continue to accumulate excessive goods, squandering available resources, while masses of people are living in conditions of misery.' Meanwhile the most powerful Christian in the world, President George W. Bush, is promoting the greatest squandering of available resources in human history. The injustice of his ethic is highlighted by the US$1.3 trillion that passes hands *every day* on the worldwide speculative-currency market. This market produces nothing; it serves only to increase the miserable gap between rich and poor. The Greens want to impose a global tax on this market. Even a tax of one-tenth of 1 per cent would raise US$1.3 billion daily. Allocated to the world's poorest billion people, this would ensure that every miserable child was given good food, clean water and a basic education.

Such a life-affirming tax would of course require international support, and President Bush would veto it. His own material riches and power are matched by his poverty of spirit towards the Earth, its biosphere and its human community. The world needs leaders who care for all people; who can feel the misery of the dispossessed; who seek power for its use in allaying misery, discrimination and unfairness; who celebrate creation and abhor the weapons that make killing easy; who appreciate the beauty of the Earth and the diversity of its life; and who, while ever vigilant and active against criminality, go out at night to see the stars, as their forebears saw them.

Such leaders will not come from the stock exchanges or oil corporations, they will come from the hearts of the people at large, borne up by the idea that respect for the Earth is the key to humanity's future security, and so to good government.

The prevailing politic uses a false script: that money

makes the world go round, that wealth is life's ultimate security, that making good means making money – put simply, that greed is good. This script, to survive, needs to condemn green philosophy. Let's hear it from Dublin columnist John Ryan who, writing in the *Sunday Independent* in 1995, had this to say about the city's Greens Lord Mayor, John Gormley:

> Is there a man or woman out there who has not concluded that these eco-friendly, one-policy politicians are almost pointlessly sad? That the Green membership is made up of crazed geography teachers and women who own too many cats? Chunky-sweatered folk who ramble at weekends, hug trees on Wednesday and spend the rest of their time polluting every conversation with scare stories about holes in the ozone layer and the greenhouse effect? I . . . smoke my head off, adore Japanese food, throw out plastic bags and am generally unconcerned about rainforests as there are very few where I live.

John Ryan typifies the nervous anger and insecurity of the materialist ostrich. There's a whiff of panic in his words, and more than a whiff of the sadness he despises. Recent studies show why. American psychologist Tim Kassar has concluded from a range of studies that people motivated by status, money or power are far more likely to be unhappy and unhealthy. British psychologist Oliver James notes that, even though individual and national wealth has soared since the 1950s, people are now between three and ten times more likely to suffer from clinical depression.

Another study, by psychologists at the University of Sussex in 2002, found that people who become involved in campaigns, strikes and political demonstrations get a psychological lift that can help them overcome stress and depression. It seems that such active involvement not only benefits the world, it returns a personal health and happiness dividend.

Money is no substitute for spirit. Lasting happiness cannot be bought or sold; it comes out of the heart rather than the pocket. Real life security and contentment come not from putting a gun in the cupboard, but from taking a role in the world's future.

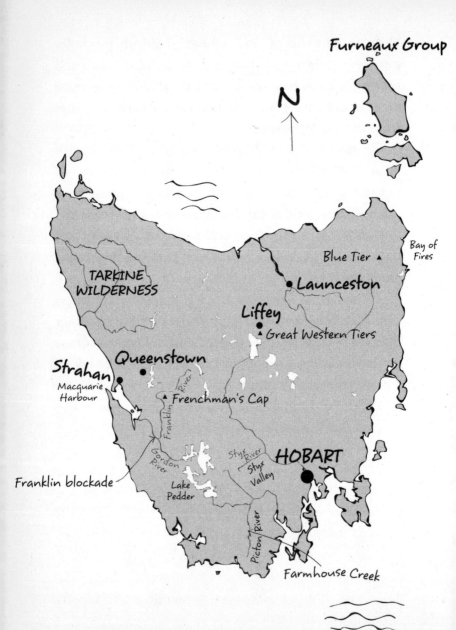

Furneaux Group

N

Bay of
Fires

Blue Tier ▲

TARKINE
WILDERNESS

Launceston

Liffey

▲ Great Western Tiers

Queenstown

Strahan

Macquarie
Harbour

Franklin River

▲ Frenchman's Cap

Gordon River

Styx River

Styx
Valley

HOBART

Franklin blockade

Lake
Pedder

Picton River

Farmhouse Creek

The Franklin Blockade

The waters of the Franklin River flow from central Tasmania's snowy highlands, through a string of gorges and lowland rainforests to the Gordon River, and then through Macquarie Harbour to the Southern Ocean. The Franklin is truly wild. It has no houses, farms, factories or fences on its banks. In its gorge country, culminating in the Great Ravine, it winds its way around the great quartzite dome of Frenchmans Cap. Its catchment area is full of wildlife and it provides, for the plucky, one of the world's great whitewater adventures.

In 1982 the Franklin was doomed. Work began on the first of a series of four dams, which were to flood almost the entire length of the river in order to harness water for hydro-electric power. This 100-metre-high dam was to sit across the Gordon River, just below its junction with the Franklin, flooding both. As Director of the Tasmanian Wilderness Society, I announced at a press conference in the gracious Hadleys Hotel in Hobart in mid-1982 that a peaceful blockade would be mounted to impede the works. We defenders of this wild, spectacular country were committed to opposing the dam 'to the last bucket of cement'. Tasmania's premier at the time, the Liberal Robin Gray, had described the Franklin as a brown, leech-ridden ditch, and at a Queenstown rally supporting the dam he put on boxing gloves to show his intentions towards the Wilderness Society. He rushed legislation through parliament to ban citizens from the riverside rainforests.

The Franklin blockade began on 14 December 1982. On the other side of the globe, the World Heritage Committee was meeting in Paris, inside a building fronted by a large throng of people holding banners reading 'Save the Franklin'. The committee voted to list Tasmania's wilderness and wild rivers, including the Franklin, in the register of World Heritage properties.

That same morning I flew over the Franklin and Gordon rivers with Norm Sanders, the Australian Democrats member of the Tasmanian parliament, in his single-engine plane. The scene below the dam site on the Gordon looked like a cross between a naval battle and a huge regatta. The cruise boats in the middle of the river were surrounded by a mêlée of red and yellow rubber rafts, blockaders' banners and flags (which also covered Butler Island), police boats, Hydro-Electric Commission encampments and vessels, and helicopters. There were also speedboats belonging to abalone divers which had carried dozens of reporters, photographers and television crews across Macquarie Harbour and up the river from Strahan, 40 kilometres away. As we flew I shed tears. For all the drama and colour on the wild river below, the odds were stacked high against us. We hoped, but could not know, that the non-violent strategy we had learned from the Quakers and from Thoreau, Gandhi and Martin Luther King was soon going to stop the dam.

Fifty-three people were arrested that day, but they weren't the first. On the previous night, four hapless rafters had floated downstream to camp at Sir John Falls in the newly forbidden forest zone. They had spent two news-free weeks rafting those wild Franklin gorges to the Gordon. The police surrounded them with a maze of searchlights and, not believing their story, promptly apprehended all four. A total of 1300 people were arrested in the following six weeks.

On 16 December, along with dozens of others from our base camp at 'Greenie Acres', west of Strahan, I went secretly aboard the old tourist launch, the *J Lee M*, captained by Denny Hamill, and was taken up to the Gordon River blockade camp. The *J Lee M* was owned by Reg Morrison, who, like Denny, had been a Huon-pine logger. They opposed the dam that threatened the forests and rivers in which they had spent years hauling punts and cutting pines. 'The Gordon River and her tributaries are my life, financially and in every other way,' Reg once said. 'If you dam the Gordon it would be like cutting off the blood to my body.' In 1939 Reg and two of his brothers had made the first recorded ascent of the Franklin River, through the Great Ravine, which they called Deception Gorge.

The *J Lee M* facilitated the blockade, carrying hundred of protesters from Strahan across Macquarie Harbour to Kelly Basin, close to where the road for the Hydro-Electric Commission was being bulldozed south to the dam site. It took hundreds more up the Gordon River to the camp near the dam site itself, playing a cat-and-mouse game with police and HEC patrols, sometimes with thirty or forty people and their packs hidden below decks. Each day, Reg – who developed the modern age of river tourism out of Strahan – captained his new cruiser the *Denison Star*, built from Huon pine, up past Butler Island to the middle of the blockade activities, giving hundreds of camera-clicking tourists an exciting bonus to their tour.

Before dawn on 17 December, our group of forty people quietly crossed the Gordon River below Butler Island on rubber rafts and walked through the rainforest on the blockaders' trail, past Perched Lake to the Lea Tree, a 3000-year-old Huon pine symbolising the ancient riverine ecosystem which was about to be drowned. I had been to the tree many times and told the others a little of its history – how it had survived because it was already too old, gnarled and knotted to be of use to the convict piners who worked these riverbanks from the infamous British penal camp at Sarah Island in Macquarie Harbour in the 1820s.

Later that morning I was arrested on a steep riverbank by a trembling young policeman to whom I gave a steadying hand. The charge was trespass: the new law of Premier Gray's stated that citizens could not 'lurk, loiter or secrete' in the wild-rivers rainforests. My companions were soon in the police compound as well. A storm blew up, and with the police launch unable to ply the waves on Macquarie Harbour, we were taken back to Strahan in a commandeered catamaran that shuddered and banged against the tempest.

We were processed at Queenstown Magistrates Court, and after refusing to sign bail conditions stipulating we must not return to the wild rivers, a busload of us were taken overnight to Hobart's Risdon Prison, arriving just as the next dawn was breaking.

On 6 January 1983, the day after I was released from Risdon, I was elected to Tasmania's House of Assembly, on a countback of preference votes for Norm Sanders in the 1982 election. After the blockade began, Norm had resigned from parliament in protest at the mistreatment of protesters. He was appalled at the drunken abuse in parliament of the 'absolutely good people' with whom he had worked to establish the Greenie Acres camp, and the next morning he got on his motorbike and rode out to the Governor to resign.

A remarkable character, Norm had blazed an environmentalist path into the redneck Tasmanian parliament in 1979. Years before, in California, he had taken part in another floating protest, against oil drilling in the sea off Santa Barbara. For four days, claiming right of way, he anchored his 14-foot fishing boat in order to prevent a 400-foot oil-drilling platform being positioned. He had also seen the deadly clashes between protesters and police in California during demonstrations against the Vietnam War. So in 1982 he was very concerned about the proposed Franklin blockade getting out of hand. He knew how ruthless the authorities could be, and foresaw danger for all of us taking part.

Despite his misgivings, Norm went to work for the Franklin blockade in a fashion few politicians would ever think to emulate: digging shit holes. As the head of the team attending the ablutions blocks at Greenie Acres, he was often ankle-deep in mud. Norm oversaw the crucial job of keeping this sprawling encampment free of disease and safe from the closure threatened by the ever-hovering health authorities. Has any other parliamentarian ever turned so much sod for so many constituents' basic needs? (In 1984 Norm was elected to the Australian Senate.)

The strength of peaceful protest lies in bringing an issue to public attention; in appealing to the people at large so that they in turn will influence politicians or developers to alter their course. But just as foot soldiers are no match for tanks, so citizens who put themselves in the path of barges or bulldozers in remote places rarely have the might, or the numbers, to stop the machines, however great their right. Their power is moral rather than physical.

In 1982 the Wilderness Society was grappling with the theory and practice of non-violent action, and how to win a 'war' through peace. Ten years earlier there had been tentative talk about obstructing the dam works that destroyed Lake Pedder National Park. Lake Pedder, a remarkably beautiful glacial lake with a 3-kilometre beach, situated high in Tasmania's southwest wilderness, was flooded to make way for a hydro-electric scheme. Though some discussed it, there had been no blockade, and the protesters, hundreds of big-hearted people who spent years campaigning to save the lake, were so distressed by their loss that they mostly did not get involved in the Franklin campaign.

Our campaign was built on the experience of Pedder. We watched as the Tasmanian chambers of business, the Trades and Labour Council, Liberals, Labor (after the downfall of the valiant Premier Doug Lowe, whose role in staving off the dam had been pivotal), and newspaper editorialists all backed once again a destructive Hydro-

Electric Commission dam, and this time we knew that having people obstruct the actual dam works would be our last option. We went for it.

In mid-winter of 1980 the Wilderness Society flew two Quakers experienced in non-violent action from New Zealand to Tasmania. They came fresh from protests against one of the Muldoon government's Think Big projects, which proposed an aluminium smelter at Aramoana, on the tidal estuary at the entrance to Otago Harbour near Dunedin. For this and the Tiwai smelter near Invercargill, dams and tunnels had been built to supply hydro-electricity (aluminium is so energy-intensive it is sometimes called 'congealed electricity'), in the process damaging picturesque rivers and lakes in the South Island's spectacular temperate wilderness. The protest was successful and the Aramoana aluminium smelter failed to go ahead.

Our weekend workshops were held at the Liffey Baptist Youth Camp, upriver from my home in northern Tasmania, where potential blockaders learned the theory and did role-plays for the prevention of violence. Violence is the bully's ally. We set up groups of six or eight, and worked out how best to handle angry workers, police and politicians.

When Premier Gray sent bulldozers from the Lyell Highway into the upper Franklin Valley in July 1982 to cut a road south through the wilderness to the dam site, we had already set up a covert working group (called the

Movement for a New Society) which met frequently at members' homes in Hobart to develop the logistics for a blockade. Scouts buried food dumps in the roadworks area. Because of our belief that the Wilderness Society's phones were tapped – a hunch later confirmed by the federal police – these meetings were held off the public record and away from our office. Similar working groups were set up in other cities around Australia and were to become crucial in training the hundreds of people who wanted to join the blockade.

Weekend meetings in the bush outside Melbourne, Sydney, Launceston, Canberra and other cities discussed how best to handle volatile or fearful fellow blockaders. Participants received booklets on their legal rights, first aid, essential equipment and campfire blockade songs. After the blockade began, everyone who arrived had to have done such a training session, or else take part in one at Greenie Acres. Each blockader joined an 'affinity group' and got to know their fellow members through long discussions about why they had come, what they feared, and how they thought the blockade should proceed. The groups were then taken either by bus from Strahan through Queenstown to blockade the access roadworks at Crotty, or up the Gordon River on the *J Lee M* to the dam site.

There was real fear in many breasts. Almost none of the 6000 who came to Strahan, let alone the 1300 who were arrested and taken to the Queenstown lockup, or the 500 who were sent to Hobart's Risdon Prison in paddy wagons, had been on the wrong side of the law before. There were added worries about jobs (Will my boss sack me? Will I ever get a public service job again?), visas (Will I be allowed into the United States or the United Kingdom if I have a police record?), and family (How will my dam-engineer father treat me when I go home for Christmas dinner?).

These fears were enhanced by the tensions in Strahan. The little town was riven into anti-dam and pro-dam camps. Brave locals like Mary Forage gave many of us bed and shelter; Harry McDermott, the mayor, stood stead-fastly for saving the river and his tourist industry, and was voted out of office on the back of a pro-dam campaign. The windows of our communications centre were smashed with rocks. One morning, most of the town's public phone services were cut by the police in an attempt to prevent us broadcasting news of the first bulldozer being brought by road to Strahan, where it was to be taken on a barge upriver to the dam site. I was knocked down and kicked by five youths wielding a wheel brace. Other visitors, includ-ing hapless tourists, were punched, spat on and abused.

The police were remarkably even-handed early on, before word was sent from Hobart headquarters to toughen up. Some arresting constables doffed their caps to show their detainees the 'No Dams' triangles stuck inside.

As news of the blockade went worldwide, with television bulletins featuring people being arrested in stunningly beautiful riverside rainforests, Robin Gray's government was faced with a national wave of public support for the protest, and it wanted sterner action. One Liberal politician demanded that interstate visitors joining the blockade be checked for head lice (if you can't win the argument, vilify the opponent), while another demanded the army be mobilised. The last time this had happened in Tasmania was during World War I, when there was a fear of riots over the conscription referendums.

In early 1983 the attitude of some senior police changed. One group of blockaders who were arrested in pouring rain faced hypothermia when left for hours beside the river. A group of women travelling in the back of a darkened paddy wagon, vomiting and with excruciatingly full bladders, were refused a rest stop on the five-hour trip in the middle of the night along the winding mountain road from Queenstown to Risdon Prison.

This was all reported by the media. In cities around Australia, street rallies were held to support the Franklin blockaders. In Hobart in February 1983 more than 20000 people thronged Franklin Square for a march through the city's central business district, in what is still the largest environmental protest ever held in Australia. There were bannered 'Save the Franklin' protests in San Francisco, London and Paris. The Franklin scored Fleet

Street headlines after the arrest in January 1983 of BBC TV's famed botanist Professor David Bellamy, who spent his fiftieth birthday in the Risdon lockup, with supporters holding a party for him outside the walls. In February Bob Hawke, the new leader of the federal Labor opposition, told 15 000 people at a Melbourne rally organised by the Wilderness Society that if Labor won the forthcoming federal election he would stop the dam. To our great delight, Hazel Hawke donned a pair of bright yellow 'No Dams' earrings.

The nation was galvanised by the fate of the Franklin. Besides the television coverage of the blockade, there was the power of Peter Dombrovskis' celebrated photograph of Rock Island Bend on the lower Franklin. It is estimated that this was printed more than a million times for the campaign. Full-page colour advertisements featuring the photograph and the caption 'Would you vote for a party that would flood this?' were placed in pre-election editions of the Melbourne *Age*, the *Sydney Morning Herald* and Brisbane's *Courier-Mail*. Old hands in Canberra tell me that this is still the most effective election advertisement they have ever seen.

On 5 March 1983 Bob Hawke's Labor Party won government, and the new prime minister's first announcement was that the dam would not be built. Premier Gray challenged the ensuing federal legislation. The subsequent High Court case kept us in high anxiety for four more months, not least when the court turned down Murray Black QC's request to submit the Wilderness Society's photo albums so that the judges could see the beauty of the rivers for themselves. Sticking strictly to matters of law, the Chief Justice ruled that the albums were inadmissible 'lest they inflame the Court's mind with irrelevancies'. We were shocked.

Some analysts predicted that we would win, but I had freshly in mind the fate of the famed Alta River in the far north of Norway, homeland of the reindeer-herding Sami people. In 1981 almost 1000 people had blockaded the road to a dam site on the Alta, and there were support protests in Oslo and all over Europe. Overcoming the blockade, in temperatures as low as -30°C, took the biggest police operation in Norwegian history, and yet the Norwegian High Court ruled seven to nil in favour of the dam.

However, the times were with us. On 1 July 1983 the High Court ruled by four judges to three that the Hawke government's legislation to protect the region's World Heritage values, thereby ensuring that Australia met its obligations to the World Heritage Convention, overrode Premier Gray's state legislation to build the dam. By eleven o'clock that morning, news flashes around the country had announced the decision, and so the plea in the blockaders' songs to 'let the Franklin run free', which had rung through the forests and jails of Tasmania, was answered.

In Tasmania it was now the dam's proponents who were shocked. Three days after the court's decision, as Premier Gray helicoptered in to visit workers along the Gordon River, the grand old Lea Tree, a Mecca for block-aders, was hacked, drilled, doused with diesel fuel and set on fire. The tree had been named after Geoffrey Lea, a casual employee of the Hydro-Electric Commission, who found it while working at the dam site and then volun-teered to work on the Wilderness Society's campaign. It burned for days with the words 'Fucking Greenie Cunts' daubed across it. No-one was ever charged with this crime.

Two months earlier, at this same campsite, police had urged me to leave the group of Labor politicians with whom, as a new member of state parliament, I was inspecting the dam works, because they feared I might be killed. The touring MPs were met by scores of work-ers brandishing lumps of wood and abusive placards directed at me. With the HEC Commissioner standing by, a circle was drawn around me on the bare ground and I was warned that if I stepped outside this I would have my 'bloody brains knocked out'. I stepped out. The two police officers present intervened and I reluctantly agreed to their request to leave the scene.

The Labor MPs then joined the vigilantes for a Devonshire tea in the mess. But what the police told me was sweeter than jam on scones: the dam builders were on strike because of my presence, and the bulldozers down by the river had been abandoned. So three hours' less construction work was done in the forests.

I have little regard for those fellow MPs, but I do not blame the workers. They were front-line victims of a remarkable campaign by big business, the unions and the Hydro-Electric Commission, and consequently by the Liberal and Labor parties, to convince Tasmanians that the dam was essential to their future wellbeing. Not unusually, this campaign ran on the slogan of 'Jobs, jobs, jobs'. Former Labor premier 'Electric' Eric Reece, who had flooded Lake Pedder, came out of retirement to lead the Association of Consumers of Electricity, which was set up to campaign for the Franklin dam. Letters were circulated to workers in factories like Australian Newsprint Mills, warning them that their futures were at stake. The editors of Tasmania's three daily newspapers joined in, claiming that the Franklin dam, due for completion in 1992, was vital for the island's economic survival and that without it Tasmania's economy would be hampered by a shortage of power. Dole queues would be extended, ending any real chance of future prosperity.

This unsubstantiated scaremongering has its parallels everywhere today. If that new tollway, petroleum plant, power station, mega-resort or forest furnace is not built, then dollars, jobs, and all hope for the future of the region will be lost. It is instructive to look at

what actually happened in Tasmania after the fateful
High Court ruling in 1983.

The projections for power demand put forward by
the Wilderness Society proved true, whereas the Hydro-
Electric Commission's projections have been shown to
be wildly high of reality. The electricity that would have
been produced by damming the Franklin was not, after all,
needed. In 1987 an associate commissioner of the HEC, Sir
Geoffrey Foot, admitted to the media that the Wilderness
Society had been right. He churlishly added, 'The fact that
they were right was because events just overtook us. Not
through accurate forecasting, but just through a fluke.'

The Wilderness Society's campaign not only saved
the Franklin River, it saved an additional $2 billion being
added to the state debt, the equivalent of $10 000 for every
Tasmanian household. The dam would have resulted in
higher power prices and consequently cost many jobs. The
$2 billion that was to be borrowed to build the dam would,
like any loan, have had to be repaid with interest. At the
rate of 10 per cent, this interest would have amounted to
$200 million annually throughout the 1980s and 1990s – a
best-case rate of 5 per cent would have cost $100 million.
This sum would have been passed on through higher electricity prices to small businesses, which are Tasmania's
biggest employers. Paying more for electricity, they would
have shed jobs to keep the books balanced.

The economic benefits to the west coast of Tasmania

have been more obvious and direct. The dam would have blighted Strahan's reputation as the gateway to the wild rivers. Nowadays more than 100 000 visitors pour into Strahan each year to see the scenic rainforest country. Wild nature is the key to Strahan's status as the most progressive, job-creating and investment-rich town in Tasmania's west. Without the dams, many more jobs have been created from the unflooded wilderness.

The icing on the cake is the $30 million restored rack-and-pinion Abt Wilderness Railway, which runs from Queenstown to Strahan. This scenic gem was pulled out in the late 1960s while Eric Reece was premier. Its rebuilding was a key part of our 1980 campaign for alternatives to the dam. The railway was reopened by Prime Minister Howard and Premier Jim Bacon in 2003, with the Franklin campaigners neither invited nor mentioned – but we were all smiling.

The saving of the Franklin and Gordon rivers bolstered Australia's pride in itself and as a world citizen. In the view of High Court Justice Lionel Murphy, one of the majority whose ruling saved the Franklin River on 1 July 1983:

> The Constitution, in its reference to external affairs . . . recognizes that while most Australians are residents of the states as well as the Commonwealth, they are also part of humanity. Under the Constitution,

Parliament has the authority to take Australia into the one world, sharing its responsibilities as well as its cultural and natural heritage.

The encouragement of people to think internationally, to regard the culture of their own country as part of world culture, to conceive a physical, spiritual and intellectual heritage, is important in the endeavour to avoid the destruction of humanity.

In 2001, two decades after the battle for the Franklin, I received a letter from the Northern Territory, which had provided some fifty of the Franklin blockaders:

Yesterday I returned home to Mutitjulu from my sixth visit to Tasmania. This time while in Tassie I took a guided eleven day trip down the Franklin River. This is something that I have been wanting to do for a while. Now I know why. It is truly a special place. Of course the political history of the River was often on our minds during the trip. I was only just being born when the struggle was going on. However I have been hearing about it all my life. The name 'the Franklin River' has always held a legendary air of mystique for me. I am sure this arises because of the magnitude of the effort that so many people put into the struggle to save the area from flooding. It was often said during our trip that 'we have a lot to thank the people for who were involved in the fight to save this place'.

Essentially that is what I am now doing, thanking everyone who gave me the opportunity to feel and experience what I just have on the River.

Back in 1979, in the early days of the campaign to save the Franklin, violinist Sir Yehudi Menuhin launched my book *The Franklin and Lower Gordon Rivers: A Wilderness Pictorial* in Melbourne. He called our fledgling Wilderness Society 'the harbingers of a new age of Noah'. He knew a lot. While we saved a raft of wild creatures from the flooding of the Franklin, a tide of human indifference has since engulfed the world and is sweeping to extinction many of the animals which, legend would have it, went two by two aboard Noah's Ark to survive the great biblical deluge thousands of years ago.

Now there is no escape. We are either part of that flooding tide of indifference, or constructers of a defiant new ark, built on intelligent compassion, to rescue ourselves and the natural world.

Because so many people cared and took action, from the dam site to the ballot box, the wild Franklin River flows free to the sea. With it flows the preservation of our hope that, through popular intervention, the Earth will be saved from utter degradation.

Global Warming:
A Global Warning

I have not seen ice on Tasmania's Liffey River since the 1970s. I think this is because of global warming.

In July 1986 Tasmania's anti-green, or, as he would have it, 'pro-development', Liberal premier Robin Gray prognosticated that 'the day I am a dictator will be the day snow falls on the GPO [General Post Office] steps'. A few days later, 8 centimetres of snow covered those steps. The white city's transport system was brought to a joyful halt and Hobartians, some skiing to work, pelted each other with snowballs in the streets. Robin Gray lost the next election.

He should have waited a bit. No snow has settled in downtown Hobart since 1986 (although there were 7 centimetres in 1951 and 15 centimetres in 1921), and while the law of averages says that it is bound to happen again, the likelihood of snow falling to sea level in Tasmania in any given year is rapidly declining.

Conversely, hot spells are becoming more frequent and prolonged. Hobart, like Sydney, New York, London, Beijing and Johannesburg, has had many record hot days, months and years since that snowy day in 1986. The 1990s was the hottest decade since instrumental records began about 150 years ago, while scientific analysis shows that in the Northern Hemisphere it was the hottest decade for at least 1000 years.

In 2003 Europe baked. London had a record-high temperature of 35.7°C. Bushfires in Portugal killed twelve people. In France as many as 15 000 people, many old and alone, died due to the heatwave. Temperatures in parts of the continent were 5°C above average for several months. In Asia too the temperature was up: a heatwave in India killed 1500 people, with some places also seeing the heaviest monsoonal rains on record.

Professor John Schellnhuber, former chief advisor to the German government and now head of Britain's Tyndall Centre for Climate Change Research commented in *The Age* on 7 August 2003 that this weather was 'absolutely unusual. We know that global warming is proceeding apace, but most of us were thinking that in 20 to 30 years' time we would be seeing hot spells (like this). But it's happening now. Clearly extreme weather events will increase.'

The former chief of Britain's Meteorological Office, Sir John Houghton, went further by equating the danger of human-induced climate change with that of international terrorism, telling *The Guardian* on 28 July 2003 that he had 'no hesitation in describing it as a "weapon of mass destruction"'. Calling for a new coalition of the willing to tackle global warming, Sir John warned that 'Like terrorism, this weapon knows no boundaries. It can strike anywhere, in any form – a heatwave in one place, a drought or a flood or a storm surge in another.'

The world's largest re-insurance company (an insurer for insurance companies), Munich Re, cites global warming as the cause of the steep rise in climate-related disasters all around the world. It gave the total cost of global natural disasters in 2003 as almost A$80 billion and 50000 lives, and forecast a 'sharp increase in insurance costs and the toll of human misery unless governments and industry take steps to reduce reliance on fossil fuels'.

Other insurance groups agree. The Insurance Australia Group points to the disproportionate changes in extreme weather which follow rising average temperatures: a 1°C mean increase can cause extreme temperatures of the sort expected once in 300 years to occur every ten years, and a 1°C mean increase in summer can lead to a 28 per cent increase in bushfires generally, with more than twice the rate of catastrophic fires.

The Sydney hailstorms in April 1999 caused insurance losses of $1700 million, IAG's greatest loss due to a natural disaster in history. IAG commissioned a study based on this storm, with early results indicating that 'small changes to atmospheric and ocean parameters' could lead to a 'megastorm that would potentially dwarf the [1999] hailstorm in both intensity and scale. Apart from an unprecedented insurance loss, a storm of this magnitude could have far-reaching implications to personal safety, disaster-relief management, and the local and national economy through business disruption.'

Worldwide, the three hottest years in history have been 2003, 2002 and 1998. According to the CSIRO, Australia warmed by 0.7°C between 1910 and 1999, and will warm another 1–6°C by 2070.

Since the Industrial Revolution began in the second half of the eighteenth century, the world has fuelled its growth in wealth, consumerism, transport and artificial comfort by burning increasing amounts of fossil fuels – coal, oil and gas. The result has been ever-increasing amounts of greenhouse gases, particularly carbon dioxide, in the air. These gases allow less heat to escape from the Earth's atmosphere. Imagine greenhouse gases as a thin layer of plastic, like the cover on a garden greenhouse: the sun's ultraviolet and visible light comes through and warms the Earth. In turn, the Earth emits infra-red radiation, which used to escape into space but is now trapped by the plastic cover and bounces back to Earth. As in a garden green-house, our planet is getting hotter.

This is not a gentle heating. The United Kingdom's Royal Commission on Environmental Pollution noted in

2000 that 'There is no precedent in recent geological history to help us understand precisely what consequences will follow . . . [T]he speed at which carbon dioxide concentration is changing appears to be unparalleled in geological history.'

Since 1800, the level of carbon dioxide in the Earth's atmosphere has risen from 280 parts per million to 375 ppm, an increase of 34 per cent. In the same period, atmospheric levels of the more potent but less voluminous greenhouse gas methane, coming out of rice fields, cattle bowels and rotting vegetation, have risen from 700 parts per billion to 1750 ppb, an increase of 150 per cent. The accumulation of these gases is acting to thicken that plastic sheet around the Earth, and the rate of accumulation is accelerating as we burn increasing amounts of fossil fuels.

Near the northwest tip of Tasmania, where the Roaring Forties bring the cleanest air in the world whistling ashore from the west, is Cape Grim. The nearest landfall to the west, across the Southern, Indian and Atlantic oceans, is Patagonia, in South America. In 1975 a United Nations monitoring station was set up on the cape to measure atmospheric pollution. Sometimes a northerly breeze blows down to Cape Grim. This causes an upwards spike in the sensitive air-pollution graph, because it brings with it air from metropolitan Melbourne, 300 kilometres away across Bass Strait.

The pollution needle falls back down when the westerly winds reassert themselves; however, the graph measuring carbon dioxide in the air at Cape Grim is relentlessly, inexorably, ineluctably going up.

As the Earth warms, so the weather goes wild. The storms which have in recent years killed thousands of people and displaced millions more are not just due to there being more people living in the most vulnerable places on Earth, in particular on the coasts. As predicted, the intensity and violence of the storms – cyclones, hurricanes, typhoons and tornadoes – have grown in line with rising temperatures. May 2003 saw a record 562 tornadoes rip through the United States. Worse storms are in store, on a wrecking scale new to human history.

With storms come landslides. Landslides result from the weight of soil being increased by water during a storm, and from the removal of trees that bind the slopes, causing the side of a mountain to be torn off. This can happen in a few minutes of chaotic breakdown, after millions of years of stability.

But these geophysical avalanches do not compare in destructive capacity to the global-warming avalanche which threatens to sweep away countries and the stability of human life on Earth as we have known it. Global warming may flip historic climate patterns, causing, within a few years, unprecedented social dislocation and destruction.

The Gulf Stream is an ocean current that sweeps north in an arc from the warm Caribbean to Norway, warming up Ireland, Britain and northern Europe. It transfers enormous heatloads via the winds off its surface, so that habitation is possible at the same latitude north as the latitude of uninhabitable Antarctica down south, where there is no warming ocean current. It is possible that global warming will actually reverse the effect of the Gulf Stream so that, as in Antarctica, the heat will be transferred out of the subarctic region, causing refrigeration in Scandinavia, Scotland, England, Ireland and Wales.

The result would be sudden Siberia in these countries. The current rise in global temperature of an average 1–2°C would be overwhelmed. What could then follow is the breakdown of this traditional bastion of democratic welfare, along with some of the world's best croplands. Millions of people in the region might have to move or face impoverishment.

Scientists know more about the Gulf Stream than about patterns in most other oceans, but it is reasonable to assume that other potentially catastrophic changes may await elsewhere in the world. As the International Geosphere-Biosphere Programme warns, 'global change is real, it is happening now, and in many ways it is accelerating. Human activities could inadvertently trigger changes with catastrophic consequences for the Earth system'. The precautionary principle should overcome our first instinct to just wait and see. We should act prudently *now* to reverse global warming, rather than sit back while politicians and business leaders, led by President George W. Bush, are out there cutting more trees on the mountainsides.

On what the Nepalese call Sagarmatha, the Tibetans Chomolungma and the English Mt Everest, the icefields have retreated 6 kilometres since New Zealand's Edmund Hillary and Nepal's Sherpa Tenzing Norgay climbed the peak in 1953. Melting glaciers in the Himalayas, Papuan highlands, New Zealand, Tibet, Greenland, the Andes, Patagonia and the European Alps are releasing huge quantities of water down their valleys to the seas. Africa's highest mountain, Kilimanjaro, has lost four-fifths of its ice since 1912. Fifteen of America's Glacier National Park glaciers have melted since the 1930s.

In a less obvious way in the years ahead, the expansion of warming oceans could cause levels to rise. Just as other elements do, water expands when it heats. There is an inertia in this: water absorbs heat more slowly than air or land, so it takes centuries for the surface heat to spread to the ocean depths. This is lucky for us, but it is a diabolical legacy for future generations. It may take four centuries for the current increase in global warming to fully express itself in expansion-related rises in sea levels, but this will occur even if we stop carbon-dioxide levels rising one more point on that graph at Cape Grim.

Last century, global warming caused sea levels to rise by 10–20 centimetres – that's up to our ankles if we are wearing shoes. It is predicted that in this century sea levels will rise by up to a metre, or as far as our crutches. Figures from the United Nations Framework Convention on Climate Change show that a 1-metre rise would submerge 6 per cent of the Netherlands, 17.5 per cent of Bangladesh, and some 80 per cent of the Marshall Islands' Majuro Atoll. Storm-produced flooding already impinges on roughly 46 million people every year, a figure that will rise with sea levels.

The worst-case scenario – one that experts say is a long way off if it happens at all – is the melting of Antarctica's icecap. Antarctica has 90 per cent of the world's ice, and it weighs so much that it depresses the Earth's southern crust by as much as 950 metres. If the ice were to melt, the crust would slowly rebound and, of itself, cause a major rise in sea levels. A full Antarctic ice-melt would cause seas to rise by 70–80 metres around the world. The Statue of Liberty, the Sydney Opera House and Big Ben would keep their tops dry in periods of calm, and the pyramids of Egypt would be islands poking out of the sea. Most of the world's great cities would have their central business districts submerged. Like Atlantis, Venice would disappear.

The spread of diseases like malaria and dengue fever will accompany rising temperatures. Dr Simon Hales of the Wellington School of Medicine and Health Resources in New Zealand says that the combination of climate change, social inequality and population increase could, by the year 2085, leave half the world's people vulnerable to the mosquito-borne dengue, or break-bone, fever. In Australia the risk would extend down the east coast beyond Brisbane.

This century is set to have an unprecedented human death toll from disasters caused by our impact on nature. While everyone faces some risk, the most vulnerable will be those in poorer countries, which produce the least greenhouse gas. A number of guiltless small island nations, like Tuvalu in the Pacific Ocean, could disappear altogether under the rising oceans. The 11 000 people of this tiny nation put their plea for survival to the Earth Summit in Johannesburg in 2002:

> We want the islands of Tuvalu, our nation, to exist permanently forever and not to be submerged under water merely due to the selfishness and greed of the industrialised world. This is why we had proposed, right from the outset, for the establishment of a legally binding framework to set targets and timeframes for renewable energy given the direct link between energy and climate change. Unfortunately our proposal never saw the light of the day, due mainly to the actions of countries that

refused to ratify the Kyoto protocol . . . Just a few weeks ago, a period when the weather was normally calm in Tuvalu, unusual waves flooded the capital island of Funafuti. A number of households were evacuated . . . It was at low tide with no strong winds when 10 metre waves washed right across the land and straight to the lagoon side. It was a very scary experience.

Prime Minister Howard rejected an appeal from the Tuvaluans for Australia, whose actions are contributing so disproportionately to their impending inundation, to take them as environmental refugees. New Zealand's Prime Minister Helen Clark, whose country emits less than half the amount of Australia's carbon dioxide per capita, promised them a place instead.

The world's wealthiest countries are the most culpable. The richest 20 per cent of the world's population burn 80 per cent of its fossil fuels, producing 80 per cent of the problem gas. The remaining 80 per cent of people produce just 20 per cent – we in the wealthy West generate sixteen times as much greenhouse gas per person as those in developing countries. In the developed countries, Australians, followed by the Americans, are the worst polluters of all. Every one of us should put that statistic in our pipe and smoke it.

Here is a picture more of greed and studied ignorance

than gloom and doom. The latter can be fixed if the former are given up. This is a moral challenge calling for a political response. And there is a good solution. Aubrey Meyer, the founder of London's Global Commons Institute, calls it 'contraction and convergence'. I would also call it 'one planet, one person, one value'. It is a just and honourable way out of the global-warming terror, and one which is every bit as much commonsense as it is a hard ask.

Stage one of the plan is to win international agreement on a level of atmospheric carbon dioxide that would ensure the Earth's ecological, social and economic future. Let's say that this is 325 parts per million, roughly halfway between the past natural level of 280 ppm and the current, human-induced level of 375 ppm.

There would follow agreements on a starting date for lowering gas emissions – say the year 2010, which would allow high-energy-consuming countries time to adjust their economies – and on a target year by which atmospheric emissions are sufficiently reduced to make that level of 325 ppm achievable. The year 2030 is realistic.

Stage two of the plan is to bestow equal status on everyone on Earth by allocating each country a level of fossil-fuel consumption based on its population. Every country would be permitted the same emission of carbon dioxide per person, to take effect in the agreed starting year (2010). Those richer communities (energy guzzlers like Australia, Japan, Canada, the United States and

Europe) unable to stick to their allocations would buy permits from the poorer countries, so keeping a lid on the total amount of fossil fuels burnt. The trading system would help close the gap between rich and poor.

Sensible and fair as this idea may be, corporate and rich-country political pressure is drowning it like a bag of unwanted kittens. The Greens' job is to rescue it. This obligation is all the more imperative when you look at what else might drown, and when you take account of the fact that the further away from the equator you get, the faster the warming will be. But to date, even the first-step Kyoto Protocol on climate change has been spurned by the Australian, American and Russian governments. The Kyoto Protocol aims to reduce greenhouse-gas production to 5 per cent below 1990 levels, but it is only a start. The global-warming situation is so drastic that it calls for reductions of 60–80 per cent below those levels.

The Howard government's behaviour risks social, economic and environmental repercussions for Australia in the future. Besides our favourite beaches being eroded, low-lying suburbs being subject to flooding, and the outlying suburbs of our biggest cities being more repeatedly burnt in bushfires, global warming threatens to damage agriculture and our ability to feed and clothe ourselves. Desertification, by droughts and bushfires, will accelerate. According to Climate Action Network Australia, 'current efforts to repair the Murray-Darling river system will be undone by 2050, with climate change causing a reduction in the river's mean flow of up to 30 percent'. By 2070, this reduction could be as great as 45 per cent.

The CSIRO's prediction that Australia will warm 1–6°C by 2070 averages out at 3.5°C this century. This would mean that, in order to enjoy the temperatures we currently experience, wherever we might live in Australia, we'd have to move a good 300 kilometres south. For those now living on the southern seaboard, that's impossible.

Other effects of global warming in Australia will be just as dire. The Great Barrier Reef has already been severely damaged by coral bleaching – that is, coral death – due to temperature rises in its shallow seas. Some scientists fear that most of the coral will be dead within two or three decades. And half of Australia's wet tropical mountain rainforests would be destroyed if we saw even a bottom-of-the-range 1°C rise in average temperature this century.

According to James Cook University's Stephen Williams, only about three of the rainforest regions' unique animal species would survive a top-of-the-range 5.8°C warming. A more modest rise of 3.5°C would see thirty species extinct and the remainder threatened. Mt Kosciuszko would lose its alpine environment. Tasmania's unique alpine pencil pines have nowhere higher to grow. Scores of familiar Australian birds

and animals, including the state emblems of Victoria
(Leadbeater's possom), South Australia (the hairy-nosed
wombat) and Queensland (the koala) would face extinction in their local habitats.

However, for some very powerful people, global
warming is bullshit. When Gary Gray began his tenure of
office as national secretary of the Australian Labor Party
in 1993, he was interviewed by *The Age*'s Jane Cadzow,
who asked him if the ALP had 'grown too bourgeois in
outlook'. He responded by saying that, as far as the environment was concerned, he was aghast at the protection
given by legislation to the habitats of things like 'flightless moths and obscure varieties of moss', to the detriment
of economic development that would create jobs. He was
also 'dismayed by middle-class hysteria over such things
as global warming', and went on to say, 'The idea of global warming is bullshit. It's pop science and yet there are
kids in schools being fed this nonsense as fact and it scares
them. What hope for the future does a young kid have if he
or she believes the world will turn into a swamp or desert
before they're 25?'

We Greens ask instead, What hope is there for
the future if we *don't* face these things? What do we
bequeath our kids if we take the option of sticking our
heads in the sand?

The Australian Financial Review of 9 January 2004
reported that global warming is expected to cause the

extinction of a quarter of the world's land animals and plants – that's more than a million species – within fifty years. This was revealed by scientific research lasting two years across four continents, headed by Professor Chris Thomas of Leeds University. The scientists found that more than 10 per cent of this loss is already irreversible, due to greenhouses gases discharged up to this point, but that a reduction in the use of fossil fuels could still save many others. But only if we act *now*.

John Howard's record of action promoting global warming is ecocidal. Mark Diesendorf of Murdoch University and Christopher Reidy of the University of Technology Sydney estimate that government subsidies for fossil fuels in Australia amount to a minimum of $6.5 billion annually, from local, state and federal funds. The Howard government contributes $3.2 billion, largely through fuel-levy rebates but also through huge grants to coal-mining companies like Rio Tinto for research and development, while funds have been stripped from excellent research into solar power. Remarkably, Australia's Chief Scientist, appointed by John Howard to advise his government, is also Rio Tinto's chief technologist.

The Prime Minister's indifference to neighbouring islanders whose world is at risk of being drowned, and his denial of Australia's responsibility to join other nations in finding a rapid alternative to a fossil-fuel economy, are also manifested in his endorsement of Regional Forest

Agreements around Australia. The RFA for Tasmania, which he signed in 1997, was effectively a death warrant for the tallest hardwood forests in the world. These forests, like those in the Styx Valley, are also the greatest carbon banks in the Southern Hemisphere. They hold huge tonnages of carbon dioxide in both the visible trees and in the root systems and organisms that live in the ground beneath the forest floor; in fact half the carbon is on or in the ground.

Through clearfelling (the rate has doubled under John Howard's prime-ministership) and burning, described as 'ecologically sustainable harvesting', vast quantities of carbon dioxide are released into the atmosphere. The tree trunks are woodchipped and exported to Japan and South Korea, where they are made into paper and ultimately dumped or burnt. Every autumn, what's left of the forests is fire-bombed in so-called 'forest regeneration' burns, and mushroom-shaped clouds extend thousands of metres into the skies. Fast-growing plantations are put in, but these absorb much less carbon dioxide from the atmosphere than do old-growth forests, and are scheduled to be cut again within a few decades.

While John Howard spent a deal of time commiserating with rural Australia during the great drought of 2002–3, he made no acknowledgement of global warming's contribution to this disaster. However, recent research has found that human-induced global warming was a key reason for the drought's severity. The research was collated in a report called 'Global Warming Contributes to Australia's Worst Drought', based on the work of Professor David Karoly of the School of Meteorology at the University of Oklahoma, Dr James Risbey of the Centre for Dynamical Meteorology and Oceanography at Monash University, and Anna Reynolds of the Worldwide Fund for Nature in Sydney.

After noting that this particular drought, which was concentrated around the Murray-Darling Basin, was Australia's worst on record, and that the average rainfall for the months of March–November 2002 was the lowest on record, the report stated that the impact of the drought was exacerbated by temperatures being 'significantly higher than in other drought years'. As a result, evaporation rates were higher, and so was the rate of loss of moisture from the soil and the drying out of vegetation and waterways. This drought was the first in Australia 'where the impact of human-induced global warming can be clearly observed'.

The higher rates of evaporation also retarded the sowing of new crops and reduced the levels of rivers and water-storage systems. These drier conditions, coupled with higher temperatures, increased the risk of bushfires. The report went on to say:

> The drought in 2002 was due to natural climate variations associated with El Niño. However, the

higher temperatures this year are not attributable to the natural variations of Australian climate alone . . . [They] are part of the overall warming trend in Australian temperatures over the last 50 years. Australian average surface temperature increased by more than 0.7°C between 1950 and 2001.

In 2001, the Intergovernmental Panel on Climate Change concluded 'most of the observed (global) warming over the last 50 years is likely to have been due to the increase in greenhouse gas concentrations'.

This was written before the devastating Canberra fires. Yet while the official report on those fires acknowledged 'the dryness of the vegetation after a prolonged, severe drought and the high volume of flammable fuel that had accumulated over time – coupled with weather conditions that were extremely conducive to fire', it ignored global warming as if it did not exist.

And the news on global warming is not getting better. In 2003 the European Union released its 'World Energy, Technology and Climate Policy Outlook', predicting a doubling of carbon-dioxide emissions between 1990 and 2030. Energy consumption will double, with the burning of oil, gas and coal all increasing. Far from reducing greenhouse gas, Europe will increase its output by 18 per cent, the developing countries by 30 per cent, and the

United States by 50 per cent. The report does not take account of recessions, other global catastrophes, riots, technological breakouts – or the Greens.

Present politics aside, Australia is beautifully placed to take a leading role in reversing this trend. From worst per-capita atmospheric polluter, we can become a world hub for rescue ecotechnology, particularly renewable energy like solar power.

In 1998 I introduced the $1.5 billion Sun Fund Bill into the Senate. A consequent Senate inquiry revealed strong support for this among emerging renewable-energy businesses and in regional areas, which stood to gain an estimated 50 000 new jobs. The bill provided for farmers and rural businesses to be paid the equivalent of ten years' diesel-fuel rebate up front in order to replace diesel generation with such options as solar hot water, solar panels for lighting, wind power or mini-hydro power. Hybrid diesel-renewable systems qualified, and investment in energy-efficient appliances was part of the package.

In my office, Margaret Blakers constructed the bill so that the Sun Fund would cost taxpayers nothing. It would be cost-neutral because it would replace a slab of the diesel rebate scheme (which is really an annual subsidy of $2–3 billion for the burning of diesel fuel). The Labor Party joined the government to vote the Sun Fund down, and my repeated efforts to get the fund backed by the Senate have failed.

Australia is the world's biggest exporter of coal. The coal industry has enormous clout in Canberra, frustrating proposals to reform energy policy. It donates to the big parties' electoral funds. Politicians, who should be acting in the interests of the people, have instead squeezed funds from research into alternative sources of power, diverted tens of millions of dollars to coal technology, and ensured that there is no European-style carbon tax in Australia. Billions of dollars have been spent on freeways instead of public transport, which is far less polluting. The destruction and burning of forests in Australia is scheduled to continue for years to come.

The good news is that none of us need be inactivated by John Howard. Ecocharity begins at home. Here are a few tips:

- Turn off the porch light before going to bed: this will prevent the release during the night of a kilogram of global-warming gases (from the coal burnt to produce the electricity)
- Recycle a large soft-drink, beer or wine bottle and save another kilogram
- Leave the car at home and walk to the shops: yet another kilogram saved
- Lobby your council to adopt the measures taken up in Queanbeyan. This innovative NSW city near Canberra gives ratepayers free water-saving showerheads and

plumbing check-ups, so saving on both water and coal-generated electricity

- Recycle and reuse, especially light metals such as aluminium. Making aluminium uses 15 per cent of Australia's entire electricity production, along with 11 per cent of its natural gas
- Plant trees. These are our respiratory partners: through photosynthesis they absorb carbon dioxide from the atmosphere and manufacture oxygen, while we humans breathe in oxygen and exhale carbon dioxide
- Check the star ratings on your next fridge, stove or washing machine: fewer stars mean you'll pay higher power prices and produce more carbon dioxide during the life of the appliance.

The Australia Institute has estimated that a tax on carbon of $25 per tonne would raise $6.8 billion per annum. Many European countries already have a carbon tax. It is the Greens' policy, through such a tax, to pay to equip every house in Australia with solar hot water and an energy-efficient fridge by 2010. These measures would cut the nation's greenhouse-gas emissions by 3 per cent and save the average household $170 a year in electricity bills. Like the Sun Fund, they would also create thousands of jobs in urban and regional Australia. To boot, there would be enough money to abolish the infamous HECS fees and assure every youngster in this clever country a free tertiary education.

In 1997 the Howard government closed down Australia's Energy Research and Development Corporation. The Greens aim to get it going again with start-up capital of $100 million per annum, and we are right behind the development of a whole slate of promising technologies, including the world's most efficient solar panels and solar hot-water systems.

Successfully tackling global warming requires an international effort beyond anything in past history. But it can be done. One beacon along the way is the success of the global effort to save the ozone layer, which blocks ultraviolet radiation from the sun. It was being broken down by the emission of chlorofluorocarbons (CFCs), synthetic chemicals used as coolants in fridges and as propellants in spraycans. The decaying impact of these CFCs on the Earth's protective ozone veil was predicted by scientists in 1974, and measured for the first time in 1984 – a hole in the veil had opened up over Antarctica. It was most pronounced in spring and exposed southernmost Australia, New Zealand and South America to increased irradiation, resulting in higher rates of skin cancer. Skin-cancer rates in Tasmania rapidly increased towards those found in tropical Queensland.

In 1987 an international treaty to phase out CFCs was signed in Montreal, to take effect from the beginning of 1989, and even tighter controls have since been agreed to. In a study led by the University of Alabama's Michael Newchurch in 2003, scientists measured a slowing of the rate of ozone loss in the uppermost stratosphere. That's a promising start towards the reversal of damage and the subsequent restoration of the ozone layer, although it will be half a century or more before nature can repair all the damage.

The question *now* is how we will respond to the much greater challenge of global warming. Just as the key to ridding the atmosphere of CFCs was the introduction of environmentally friendly substitutes, the key here lies in finding substitutes for fossil fuels and for the processes that produce greenhouse gases. The whole world, Australia included, must agree to a timetable and to tough, clear laws to achieve this.

And it is achievable. The solar energy hitting the Earth is about 10 000 times our total energy use. To put it another way, the solar energy that hits Australia alone in one average summer is comparable to the entire world's total annual energy use.

The Sun gives us life but it is a fiery neighbour. Keeping the Earth's atmosphere healthy is our insurance against being seared. Burning coal, oil, gas and forests at an ever-increasing rate is not only collective folly, but a declaration to our children that this generation's powerbrokers just did not care. They need replacing with the Greens.

One Person, One Value

Some people think that the Earth is here for humans to subdue and exploit. Others believe the planet would be better off without people at all. We Greens pursue the goal of a global community living in balance with the Earth, respecting it as the only life-giving speck in the universe, so far as we know. The green that affords us life.

A century ago there were less than 2 billion people on the planet. Now there are more than 6 billion. It is predicted that by 2050 the global population will peak at 9–10 billion. After that it will level off or gradually decline; the proven trend is that as people become better educated and wealthier, they choose to have smaller families or no children at all. Overpopulation can lead to population collapse, eliminating the rich as well as the poor through disease, starvation and civil insurrection. As the population increases ahead of the planet's ability to provide resources, so the risks for all of us grow.

The market fundamentalists who rule the world are aghast at the idea of static populations. Pivotal to their idea of a healthy economy is growth, which depends on growing markets. This, in turn, depends to a large extent on growth in population. The fears on the part of government and business in Australia over predictions of population stasis are little different from those all around the world. Zero population growth equates to stalled economic growth, and gloom.

The fundamentalists also worry about the market consequences of there being more old, nonproductive people and fewer young, productive people. Average incomes, they assert, will fall. Grandparents are a useless burden and there will be fewer taxpayers to support old-age pensions. This dollar-value view of society subjugates more humane values, and makes the market master of the common good, rather than the other way round.

The Vatican and the White House are both intervening, via the United Nations and world forums on population, to curtail funding that allows women and men in poorer countries access to contraceptives and sterilisation. They seek to remove the right of people to decide for themselves how few children they will raise and how much poverty they will endure. The Vatican says the Earth can sustain 40 billion people. This raises the question of what then? Four hundred billion? Four trillion? The world's human population already lives in huge sedentary herds, like no other mammal before; there are forty cities of more than 5 million people each, and greater Tokyo has 27 million. Where does a city start and end? Chongqing municipality in China has 31 million people.

This global population is straining the larder. A huge proportion of the world's food and water is being purloined by *Homo sapiens* at the expense of all the other species that depend on the same finite resources for survival. One-fifth of the world's population consumes four-fifths of its resources. For the poor to catch up with the rich – and, with the possible exception of the world's 300 million indigenous people still living their traditional lives, they very much want to – five times as much resources would be required. And when the population expands to at least 9 billion by 2050, consumption will suck up half as much again. Multiply five by one and a half: in less than fifty years' time we'll need 7.5 times as many resources as we use now. This simply cannot happen. We will not find two or three more Earthlike planets, so we are left with the option of the over-consumers among us pulling our belts in so that the poor can live like us.

Some people put hope in technological breakthroughs in food, housing, energy, transport and recycling. But it's obvious that a techno-fix alone cannot remove the dangers of what American scientist Paul Ehrlich described more than thirty years ago as 'the population bomb'.

Population crush in any species invites a plague.

In the 1990s virulent, drug-resistant strains of malaria and tuberculosis killed millions of human beings. Tens of millions of young parents and children have died or are dying from HIV/AIDS. The spectre of a disastrous global pandemic, such as a mutation of the 2004 bird flu, increases with our human population and the cramming together of the birds and animals we eat.

According to the International Labor Organization, 3 billion people survive on US$2 a day or less, and there are now 180 million people without jobs. (In 1990 the latter figure was 100 million.) Starvation stalks millions of the world's poorest people. While garbage bins from Boston to Brisbane are full of discarded food, in the backblocks of Dhaka and Pyongyang infants and nursing mothers are dying from having too little to eat or polluted water to drink.

The issue of population cannot be divorced from inequality in living standards, or from world security. Inequity breeds anger. The Internet, radio and television make it very evident to the poor, as well as the rich, just who has wealth and who has nothing, and the availability of powerful technologies, including weapons, gives ready firepower to the dispossessed. Inevitably, one person's technology becomes every person's technology. In a world that trades on armaments, being rich at someone else's expense can be very self-defeating. Inequality, armaments and anger are the ingredients of terror's cocktail, yet the world continues to gather and shake them. The New York Stock Exchange, which leads world markets and whose director was given a US$130 million (AU$200 million) pay-out in 2003, disregards destructive inequities even as it fosters destructive technologies.

The world will always need policing. Villainy is part of society, but when the laws themselves help create villainy, when you have a world order that fosters extreme inequality and turns its back on avoidable suffering, when you have a minority flaunting their extravagance while millions go without, then the circumstances are set for broadscale retaliatory action beyond anyone's control.

I am not sure that Prime Minister Howard understands this. In 2000 I wrote to him and asked what he thought of the fact that the wealth of the world's 358 richest tycoons equalled the income of the world's poorest billion people. Here is his reply: 'It is a dramatic statistic, which draws attention to disparities in wealth between rich and poor countries. Australia must bear those disparities in mind when formulating policies.'

This is such a craftily worded commitment to absolutely nothing that I'm inclined to believe the Prime Minister wrote it himself.

For global governance to take equal account of the safety and wellbeing of all citizens – and to aim at the fair distribution of wealth and opportunity, including fair trade – a global parliament with a democratic power base is needed. Such a parliament would afford everyone on Earth the democracy and freedom that President George W. Bush espouses. 'I love free speech!' he told us all in Canberra in 2003. But he does not love the idea of a global ballot box near as much. It would speak to him more freely and powerfully than any of his advisors.

President Bush, Prime Minister Blair and Prime Minister Howard advocate democracy almost as stridently as they defend the market. Their concept of economic globalisation dominates international forums, but for them democracy is to be kept within national limits. Global democracy is not on the agenda. Many people have argued the case for true global democracy over the years. I raised it in a speech to the National Press Club in 1997, but it rated nary a scribble in the press.

In June 2003 I raised it again in the parliament, putting a motion that the Senate support global democracy based on the principle of 'one person, one vote, one value', and that it support the vision of a global parliament which would empower all the world's people, equally, to decide on matters of international significance. The motion was denied by a vote of forty-five against, with only my fellow Greens senator, Kerry Nettle, joining in to support it. Twenty-nine of the House's 76 senators weren't even present, which says a lot about how relevant this issue is held to be by both Liberal and Labor. Before the division on the motion, an opposing senator, who is way above par in terms of social conscience and humaneness, chided me with 'Bob, don't you know how many Chinese there are?'

The transition to world democracy will need to be democratic itself, with nations retaining control of their own affairs but opting in to global governance in matters of global significance. This is not a new idea. Nations queued to join the World Trade Organization, with its one-nation, one-vote system, although this is a limited formula, and led to a boycott by the United States and Europe in the face of a collective vote by poorer countries seeking fairer trade terms at the meeting in Cancún, Mexico, in 2003. There is already a de facto world governance by multinational corporations which far outweighs the United Nations in terms of economic clout and influence and which leaves a lot to be desired in terms of democracy. History has shown that democracy increases the security of everyone, although of course not everyone is prepared to admit that security requires sharing rather than hoarding everything from political power to resources.

Population and global governance cannot be considered in isolation from the plight of other species. More people on the planet means smaller numbers of other creatures, yet human life depends on plants, animals, insects, fish and fungi. Nature's vast variety affords us life itself. Even so, our natural treasure chest is being rapidly destroyed: forests are bulldozed, fleets are devastating fishing grounds, and virulent pests adept at competing against human interests are being spread around the world, displacing local species on which we might depend. We have only scratched the surface when it comes to knowledge of the nutritional and pharmaceutical properties of many threatened species.

This is not an inadvertent process. Corporations who raze native forests, for example, reverse the precautionary principle and challenge their critics to prove they are causing extinctions. They do not survey ecosystems before they invade and plunder them. Thousands of insect species, for instance, are being eliminated unrecorded and unstudied, their utility as well as their beauty erased forever.

If the Vatican's 40 billion people, which would require an extra ten planets' resources, is okay, what will happen when that figure is achieved? To those who oppose family planning, stopping at 40 billion would be immoral, and for the market fundamentalists it would be economically irrational. By their logic, the future should be left to run its course until there is just enough space for people to stand side by side on their allotted half a square metre – just enough room to copulate and hold aloft the next generation! Fortunately the Pope's Italy has defied the encyclicals against contraception and has the lowest birthrate in Europe.

And where Italy has gone, the world is sure to follow. British journalist Martin Woollacott, writing in *The Guardian Weekly* of 21–27 August 2003, reported an observation by Professor Robert Cassen from the London School of Economics on India's declining rate of population increase. Cassen noted that two-thirds of this decline was due to uneducated people deciding that their children would have a better chance of getting an education if they had fewer of them. Woollacott goes on to discuss the problem of the 'disproportionate class of ageing people' that results when population growth finally comes to an end, as it inevitably must in any society, and writes:

> His [Cassen's] is an insight that seems obvious enough, yet it is rarely part of the discussion. This inevitable change cannot be staved off by natalist policies such as those practised by most European societies, and by the Soviet Union in the past. It can be made somewhat easier by the right kind of family policies, by extending the retirement age, and by a judicious approach to immigration.

Australia's birthrate, as is the case in other rich countries, has had a healthy fall, and already our main source of population growth is immigration. Should we be keeping our population static at the 20 million mark by lowering immigration levels (an annual average of 70000 over the last ten years and currently more than 100000 a year) to match emigration (approximately 40000 a year)? The answer is no. We have to accept our responsibility as part of the global community. We cannot pull up a drawbridge and turn our back on the world; let us take a small share of the world's desperate people until the global crisis is past. We can do a lot more to hasten that day: through overseas aid to lift people above the poverty line and ensure access to family-planning and basic education; by promoting global democracy; and by supplanting market fundamentalism, which ties market growth to population growth, with fair trade and sustainable economic policies. The World Trade Organization can help by abolishing agricultural barriers, including subsidies, through which the wealthier nations undercut the poorer nations in world trade.

Australia is a middle-order country in terms of global influence, but on top of the world list in terms of affluence and resources available per person. Governments are wise to regulate immigration from year to year, rather than setting a statutory figure. Changing external factors (such as the Tiananmen Square massacre of 1989, after which the Hawke government allowed more than 10000 Chinese students to stay on in Australia) and internal factors (immigration levels may be reduced in times of economic recession and high unemployment) must be catered for. Regarding who comes here, we Greens call for greater emphasis on humanitarian considerations, such as reuniting families, rather than the wealth of applicants.

The mix of Australia's current immigration program is deliberately skewed towards skilled or rich people – who are allocated thousands of places based on their wealth – and away from the poor. The former are needed in their own countries to help development, while the poor are more deserving of a chance to prosper in Australia.

Even the modest population increase that current projections allow for by the middle of this century – some 5 million more for Australia as the world population grows by at least 3 billion – has to be considered in terms of its impact on the Australian environment, such as the further demands made on soil, water and biodiversity. The global market sees our continent as an export dynamo for grain, meat, minerals and energy, as well as a major tourism destination. That market pressure will sorely test democratic processes, including those of the Greens.

It has done so already. Some fellow environmentalists want zero population growth now. However, I am a big-G Green, for whom human welfare is an essential political consideration. Our aim must be to accommodate both social and environmental wellbeing; we need to design a future in which the national and global environments survive as well as possible the population increase that lies ahead. Future generations will be the judge of how well we do this.

Unlike the old parties, we Greens believe that environmental laws with real teeth are the best protection for the environment. Laws based on the recognition that environmental degradation is at least as damaging to society as white-collar crime – and in the long-term far more damaging – will do a lot more to preserve Australia's natural heritage and security than will the concept of instant zero population growth in a sea of unfairly treated humanity.

The Greens abhor the policy of expelling as many as possible of those thousands of warm-blooded and indisputably enterprising refugees who have been locked up behind razor wire in the Australian desert in recent years and denied internationally accepted justice. For far less than the hundreds of millions of dollars – and the environmental degradation – that their internment has cost taxpayers, these people could have by now been productive, happy citizens in our nation of immigrants. I have committed even more of my work as a senator to them than I have to keeping the chainsaws out of the forests.

All 6 billion of us world citizens share the past and the future. Whereas our common past, out of Africa, saw a global diaspora of humankind, our common future depends on a global coming together and consensus, resulting in a more equitable distribution of the Earth's largesse. When Africa, which gave all of us the wealth of life, has that debt returned, the world will have come of age.

The will to achieve a strong, global governance that would ensure humanity's future might be lacking in the halls of power, but it is not absent at other levels. In 1992 the Union of Concerned Scientists spearheaded an appeal to politicians everywhere on the problems facing the Earth. Among the 1700 signatories to their World Scientists' Warning to Humanity were most of the Nobel Prize-winners in the sciences.

If you've never heard of this remarkable statement, don't blame yourself. Had it been predicting the collapse of the stock market rather than of global living systems, it would have made front-page headlines in the wealthy world's press. But this being the age of market fundamentalism – and also the age of mind-block, denial, displacement behaviour, and repression of information in the interests of short-term capital gain – it went largely ignored by the media. Money, not the planet; the ersatz, not the real, make better news.

The scientists pointed to the pressure of population growth on the Earth's atmosphere, water resources, oceans, soil, forests and species – the 'interdependent web of life' – and warned that, left unchecked, such growth would subvert any attempts at creating a sustainable future. They then outlined a course of simultaneous action crucial for averting disaster, including the cessation of excessive burning of fossil fuels, an end to deforestation and the destruction of agricultural land, efficient management and use of natural resources, population stabilisation, the reduction and eventual elimination of poverty, sexual equality and the right to independent reproductive decisions. The scientists asserted that such action amounted not to

> altruism, but enlightened self-interest: whether industrialized or not, we all have but one lifeboat. No nation can escape from injury when global biological systems are damaged. No nation can escape from conflicts over increasingly scarce resources. In addition, environmental and economic instabilities will cause mass migrations with incalculable consequences for developed and undeveloped nations alike.

It is a wan hope that the older political establishment – either the conservative or social-democratic parties – can make the necessary transformation to such enlightened self-interest. Being so indentured to the predominance of market-oriented policies, they are incapable of reform from within. As the great German Green Petra Kelly, who had worked with both the Democrats in the United States and the Social Democrats in Europe, told me at Liffey in 1984, 'They put on their green spots in opposition and shed them in government.' I think this is the reason why the Greens have arisen by spontaneous combustion around the world. While there are no angels in politics, at least we are with those 1700 world scientists. Where the hidebound old parties will not meet the scientists' call, we can and will.

As well as reconsidering the market-obsessed economic approach, it would be very healthy for our consumerist society to relax a little about death. There is an undeniable link between the two: death, the disperser, does not sit well with a life ethic of accrual.

A person's life, wrote Thomas Carlyle in 1837, is 'a little gleam of time between two Eternities'. That gleam begins at birth and ends in death. Death is essential to love and to life, and to our purpose in life. It is nature's way of ensuring that the whole fabric of the planet evolves and continues to alter, seeking out its full potential. It seems incredible to our spirits that life has such a contrary and overriding factor. From inside ourselves, subjectively, death is frighteningly negative. Woody Allen put it this way: 'I don't want to achieve immortality through my work; I want to achieve immortality through not dying.' Immortality not being on offer, most of us have evolved to deny our mortality. Otherwise we could not happily go about daily life.

Objectively, however, death is not at all negative. Evolutionary progress needs a clearing mechanism for the rapid turnover of generations on Earth. Death is an essential part of the search for life's ultimate possibilities. Thanks to death, you and I exist. The alternative to death is for us never to have existed. Death is life's bargain.

Each generation has moved a little closer to being us. We, in turn, will die in order to allow the species to evolve through future generations. (Hopefully this will include an increase in commonsense, so that this species will survive!) But this process has kicked up a shortcoming or two, not least that denial mechanism whereby, as a necessary aid to individual survival, we avoid thinking of our own deaths. Powerful but analytically impoverished people are incapable of recognising that their own actions, be they declaring war or pillaging the environment, can lead to a catastrophe which will take them with it.

We all have this fault to some degree. It is our Armageddon flaw, and it leaves our rudimentary instincts dangerously unbraked. It is unnervingly proportional to one's thirst for political power and wealth. It has enabled some of the world's cleverest people to fiddle with computers in bunkers, ready to unleash nuclear war. It is why the presidents of the United States and Russia never travel without their black bags to authorise a nuclear strike, and it was fundamental to the twentieth century's Cold War philosophy of mutually assured destruction. It is balanced by and in tension with human compassion, our empathy for other beings, a quality which can be inversely proportional to one's thirst for political power and wealth.

Every human being is a unique variant on a very successful mammalian formula: *Homo sapiens*, the improved model of *Homo erectus*. Every bit of our physical selves – eyelashes, nostrils, anus and armpits – has been found good for life on Earth and replicated over and over again. So has the way we chew, sneeze, smile and itch; the way we smell roses, experience shock or orgasms, and coo at babies. But no previous generation has had the fate of the Earth in its hands. That makes ours different. Our circumstances, although not we ourselves, are markedly different from those of all our forebears.

After the Big Bang, 14–15 billion years ago, it took billions of years for the Earth to precipitate out of the cosmos, to round off, cool, and get into its orbit around the sun. It took 1–2 billion years for the relationship between air, sea and land to become just right so that life could begin in the primordial sludge – perhaps by way of some Earth-crashing asteroid carrying the primitive chemical building blocks for life. Out of the mud and into the ocean, life then moved ashore. This biological evolution was much faster than geological evolution.

The evolution of human consciousness – from 'the world exists' to 'I exist and am happening' to 'I exist and have a responsibility for what happens to me and the world' – is much faster still. Our awareness is unfolding very rapidly.

But the Armageddon flaw remains. While our power to change the Earth has evolved, along with an accompanying sense of responsibility for it, the instinct for self-preservation can readily override our will to ensure the wellbeing of humanity as a whole. Individuals, or small groups of them, have gained the power to destroy millions of others, and this power – nuclear, biological, chemical – is becoming attainable for more and more people – presidents, businessmen and terrorists.

Evolution may be likened to an endless relay, with each generation passing the baton of potential to the next. In the twenty-first century every single one of us in the global community holds a little of this baton, which has already been passed on millions of times. Will we collectively drop it?

Many teams of species are in the relay and many have already dropped their batons. The dinosaurs lost theirs when one or more huge meteors struck the Earth some 65 million years ago, creating tidal waves, darkness and cold, and destroying their food supply. One moment the dinosaurs were predominant, the next they were extinct. When they succumbed, a furry little mouselike animal, with more than 90 per cent of the same genes as us, was there too. This ancestor mammal survived the catastrophe and began passing its baton of evolving genes on to us.

In recent centuries *Homo sapiens* has been the prime cause of other species dropping their batons. The dodo, moa, mammoth, passenger pigeon, thylacine and Stellar's sea cow have all been bumped into extinction, the latter within just twenty-seven years of its 'discovery' by Europeans in the North Pacific.

With our new creations of weaponry, genetic manipulation, computers, nanotechnology and conscience-free robotic servants, the possibility that our human lineage will bump itself off as well is growing. How can we ensure human survival in an age of weapons of mass destruction? We must develop universally agreed laws which clamp down on both the weapons and weapons research.

Scientists have a key role to play in developing and maintaining the ethics and global vision for these laws. In 2001, celebrating the hundredth anniversary of the Nobel Prize, 150 past winners from across the disciplines issued a statement that read in part:

> The most profound danger to world peace in the coming years will stem not from the irrational acts of states or individuals but from the legitimate demands of the world's dispossessed. Of these poor and disenfranchised, the majority live a marginal existence in equatorial climates. Global warming, not of their making but originating with the wealthy few, will affect their fragile ecologies most. Their situation will be desperate and manifestly unjust.
>
> It cannot be expected, therefore, that in all

cases they will be content to await the beneficence of the rich. If, then, we permit the devastating power of modern weaponry to spread through this combustible human landscape, we invite a conflagration that can engulf both rich and poor. The only hope for the future lies in cooperative international action, legitimized by democracy.

The Greens take this challenge to be pivotal in politics. Around the world we are working for a robust combination of ecology (this word, which derives from the Greek for 'house', means 'understanding the house') and economy (managing the house). The Earth is our house, and good management of it must be built on a good understanding: good economy is dependent, in the first place, upon good ecology. The Greens understand that the wellbeing of coming generations – who have no say or vote in this – is directly dependent upon what we do now. Rather than simply asking what is needed to win the next election, we Greens ask, Will people a hundred years from now thank us for what we are doing?

In an era of me-now market fundamentalism this is a revolutionary question, one which shorthands the difference between the politics of green and greed. In its answer rides the future wellbeing of the world.

The Styx Valley:
The Valley of the Giants

Half of the planet's forests and woodlands are already gone.

When the 1992 Earth Summit in Rio de Janeiro concluded that the degradation of the world's forests required 'urgent and consistent action', participating countries agreed that this should begin with 'national policies and strategies . . . for the management, conservation and sustainable development of forests and forest lands', including the conservation of the wildlife in those forests.

In Australia, as in many other countries, that proposal came home only to be axed. Ten years on, forests covering an area greater than the size of Florida, or England and Wales combined, or two Tasmanias, are being cleared around the world *every year*. And the rate is going up, not down. The worst devastation is occurring in Brazil, Indonesia and Sudan, and the list of the worst ten countries is made up of poorer countries, with one exception – Australia, which jostles with Bolivia for fifth-worst position. Tasmania's forests and Queensland's woodlands are bearing the brunt of the destruction. In Queensland, five years after the Rio Earth Summit, woodlands were being cleared at a rate half as fast again.

In November 1997 Prime Minister Howard (one of the few world leaders to duck the next Earth Summit in Johannesburg in 2002) flew to Tasmania to sign the island's Regional Forest Agreement. This death warrant, also signed by the Tasmanian government, guaranteed the logging companies the right to exploit more than a million hectares of forest on public lands, and nearly as much on private lands.

I have a vivid recollection of John Howard's arrival at Forestry Tasmania's offices, near the village of Perth, to sign the RFA. With sixty other Tasmanians, some holding placards reading 'Save Tassie's Forests', I was standing in the leafy entrance laneway when the prime-ministerial car approached, with bodyguards walking on either side. As the car pushed through the crowd, I stood my ground and was knocked over by the bodyguard holding the handle of the prime minister's passenger-side door. 'Oh Senator,' he cried as he went down too, landing on top of me. A gun fell out of his pocket, spinning around on the asphalt next to my head. He grabbed it back before I could give him a hand.

John Howard looked ashen. Safely inside, he predicted that the RFA would create 1000 new jobs and he gave the logging industry $80 million of taxpayers' money to achieve this.

Since 1997, woodchipping of Tasmania's forests has increased by more than 2 million tonnes to 5 million tonnes per annum, but instead of 1000 new jobs being created, hundreds of jobs have been shed. The Tasmanian ALP and unions nevertheless support John Howard's agreement. Woodchips, the product of this wasteful industry, are the dollar-sized pieces churned out of the mills. Like enormous pencil sharpeners, the mills shred the tree trunks into piles of chips for transport to the paper mills of Japan, China and South Korea.

The Styx Valley in central Tasmania is known as the Valley of the Giants because it is home to the world's tallest hardwood forests. Under the RFA, large tracts of forest, called coupes, are being smashed out of its hillsides, and new roads, subsidised by taxpayers, are being built deeper into its groves. Victorian tree-hunter Brett Mifsud has measured the height of the gnarled Mount Tree in the tiny Andromeda Reserve at 96 metres. The previous king of the measured trees (their botanical name, *Eucalyptus regnans*, means 'eucalypt king') was 92 metres, standing a few kilometres west in the even smaller Big Tree Reserve.

These trees, if they were rising from Port Jackson's

water level, would spread their branches from the deck level of the Sydney Harbour Bridge high up into the arch, and their tops would soar far above the sails of the Opera House. When the Wilderness Society and the Greens began campaigning for the Styx Valley to become a national park, Forestry Tasmania, the state's silvicidal authority, rejected the idea. Instead it put some new signs and boardwalks into the postage-stamp-sized reserves around the tallest measured trees.

But the forests are much more than trees. In these ancient eucalypts, and in the rainforest trees and forest floor below, is a vigorous array of wildlife. One morning I was parked in the Styx forest when a yellow, caterpillar-like creature dropped onto my car. It looked like a grub but moved quickly, waves of motion passing down its 2-centimetre body, leaving behind a trail of silky thread like that of a silkworm. I had no idea what it was. There may be hundreds of such invertebrates, unknown to science, in Tasmania's forests, or even in each valley of the forests. Of the hundreds, a few will be so rare as to face extinction when the area is logged. Maybe the little yellow wriggler on my car was facing such an exit. I fought off the urge to put it in a matchbox to see if science did know about it.

The Styx Valley is full of wallabies, potoroos (small kangaroos whose shape, like that of the now defunct Concorde, helps them dart through the undergrowth), marsupial rats, bandicoots, echidnas and possums (brush-tails, ringtails, gliders and pygmy possums). The trees provide nesting sites for wedgetail eagles, Tasmania's white-feathered and red-eyed goshawks, yellow-tailed black cockatoos, green rosellas, and pink rainforest robins. After dark, owls call from the trees, and in summer bats use their sonar devices to catch insects in the evening air. Tasmania's bats nest only in trees. The waters of the Styx River are home to trout – both native and introduced species – platypuses, yabbies and cormorants.

The biggest trees are mainly *Eucalyptus regnans*, which have brown or grey bark at the bottom but then long, smooth, dappled white trunks. There are other eucalypts too, including the statuesque *Eucalyptus delegatensis* (named after the town of Delegate on the Snowy River in New South Wales) and *Eucalyptus obliqua*. These species are also found in the southeast of mainland Australia. Many of the giants have dead branches on top. Forestry Tasmania says that these are senescing (ageing), and so thinning on top – rather like me. The reason for this, in the case of the trees, is not certain. Maybe they are just old. Maybe they shed their most dispensable branches during hard times in the last century or so. In a bad drought, trees can react to water shortage by depriving those leaves they have to pump hardest to supply – the ones at the top. Maybe some of the trees were hit by lightning.

Beneath the scattered eucalypts grows fabulously green rainforest. During the campaign to save the Franklin River in 1982, TV's 'Pommy botanist' David Bellamy made Tasmania's rainforests famous by chewing on some of the leaves and explaining that dinosaurs had chomped the very same species of trees more than 65 million years ago. The rainforest's species, which include myrtles (*Nothofagus cunninghamii*), sassafras, leatherwoods, celery-top pines and the radiant tree fern, have graced the Earth for hundreds of millions of years – far longer than the more recently evolved eucalypts.

In early summer, yellow wattles, red waratahs and white Christmas trees (*Prostanthera lamiaceae*) colour the creek banks. The forests also contain stinkbush (*Zieria arborescens*; stinkbush is an appalling misnomer because these white-flowered lovelies exude the most acceptably nostril-clearing aroma), dogwoods, musk trees, and a dazzling array of ferns, ground orchids, mosses and fungi – red, blue, orange and green – which are at their best in late autumn.

The Maydena Range to the north of the Valley of the Giants is often snow-covered in winter, and snow sometimes dusts the giant eucalypts in the valley below. During the coldest weeks of the year, the loftier, dolerite-topped Snowy Range to the south is blanketed with snow. Down from the Snowy Range and from Mt Mueller at the western end of the valley, tumble the South Styx and

Styx rivers. Many other streams join them. Some have beautiful waterfalls, like the Julia Falls on a tributary of the Andromeda Creek, only a couple of kilometres from the Styx River.

The overhangs of cliffs once made ideal camping spots for Tasmania's Aboriginal people. Before the end of the last ice age 10 000 years ago, there were glaciers hundreds of metres thick on Tasmania's loftier ranges, grinding their way down into the valleys. During this period the forests contracted down to warmer places along the Derwent River. The Styx Valley was much more open, with grasslands and grazing marsupials.

On some of the lower slopes I have picked up sandstones studded with shells and seaweed fossils from 200–300 million years ago, when the hillsides were part of the seabed. Some of the fossilised rocks have tumbled down to the river as it has slowly eroded the hillsides, and nowadays they help make up its shingle banks. Further up the valley there is limestone and a giant sinkhole near the river.

Aboriginal occupation of the Styx Valley ebbed and flowed with the ice. Curiously, the contraction of the forests when things got colder made the valley much more comfortable for people, with those open grasslands downhill of the ice providing excellent hunting grounds. As the rainforests moved back in during warmer times, the people moved out, keeping tracks across the region that linked the grasslands on either side.

When Tasmania's Aborigines saw Abel Tasman sailing off the coast in 1642, the older rainforest trees, tree ferns and great eucalypts now growing in the Valley of the Giants were already there. When the British military and convict settlements appeared in Hobart and Launceston in the first decade of the nineteenth century, many of these trees were in their youthful prime. Today's old giants were young giants.

The Styx Valley, like the Tyenna Valley to its north (where the villages of Maydena and Westerway now nestle), was eyed for a railway route from Hobart to the west coast in the 1880s, and by prospectors for osmiridium (used in pen nibs) in the 1920s. Other prospectors came up the river looking for gold. They got more cold than gold.

Then came the loggers.

The first track was cut from Fitzgerald, the original end-of-the-line village before Maydena was set up as a loggers' settlement by Australian Newsprint Mills (ANM). The track wound over the western flank of the Maydena Range, along the route of the modern Styx Road. Here and there by the sides of the road, old rotting stumps still show notches where the sawyers inserted their foot boards before the trees were cut down by crosscut saw in the early 1900s. In that pre-chainsaw age, sawlogs for housing-frames, walls and floorboards (some were probably shipped to Melbourne) were in keen demand.

ANM wanted the trees for its pulp and paper factory on the Derwent River, near New Norfolk, but these days the mill, now owned by the Scandinavian company Norske Skog, is not the scourge of the Styx Valley's old-growth forests.

In 1970 the woodchippers arrived. Figures from the Australian Bureau of Statistics show that since 2000 as little as 4 per cent of Tasmania's public forests has ended up as sawn timber. Less still is made into veneer. These have become small by-products of the low-earning export woodchip industry, which since 1970 has seen the closure of more than a hundred local sawmills and the loss of more than 5000 jobs. Nowadays the Valley of the Giants is being slaughtered by unbelievably powerful machinery – bulldozers, D9s, chainsaws, B-double trucks and cable-logging rigs – which is razing Tasmania's forests at the greatest rate in history for the lowest return in history, with the fewest jobs in history.

Forestry Tasmania has declared itself ready to protect those trees which are taller than 85 metres. If the trees are 82, 83 or 84 metres high, down they come. The woodchippers are destroying millions of wild trees around Tasmania, as each year 150 000 log trucks carry 5 million tonnes to the woodchip mills. Forestry Tasmania also promises to protect trees with a girth of more than 18 metres (such a tree would not fit into your average-sized bedroom), but in April 2003 one of its fires got away and burnt El Grande, Australia's biggest tree – by volume, although not by height – in the Florentine Valley north of the Styx. The tree was officially declared dead in December 2003, after it failed to regenerate in spring.

A 2004 Newspoll, commissioned by the group Doctors for Forests, showed that 85.4 per cent of Australians want the federal government to stop the logging of Tasmania's old-growth forests. Yet the forests continue to be logged for woodchips at double the rate and volume of all the mainland states combined. More woodchip mills are on the drawing board.

As a rule of thumb, Tasmanians get $10–12 per tonne from the woodchip corporations for their trees, which have taken centuries to grow. Within weeks, the corporations get some $100 per tonne for the woodchips. A few months later, Japanese millers get more than $1000 per tonne for the paper. So at each stage there is a tenfold mark-up. Tasmanians get 1 per cent of the price the Japanese papermakers take.

Labor and Liberal politicians in Hobart and Canberra voted unanimously for the Regional Forest Agreement that guarantees this sell-out. They should take note of the fact that in February 2001 West Australians elected a new Labor government with a Doctors for Forests member in the lower house and five Greens in the upper house in order to end most old-growth woodchipping in that state.

Politicians are generally frightened of forests. One

exception was Graham Richardson, Minister for the Environment in the 1980s Hawke government. He came to look at Tasmania's forests and was so impressed he helped save the fraction that is now in national parks. Prime Minister Hawke refused to visit, saying, 'I saw what happened to Richo.' Paul Keating also spurned invitations to visit the forests he could have protected. In 1996, just after John Howard became prime minister, I asked him over a cup of tea in Sydney if he would visit Tasmania's forests. He wouldn't: but a year later he signed the RFA that condemned them, sight unseen. I have no doubt that the deep bond connecting humans to nature is buried within every prime minister's breast, even John Howard's, but when that bond threatens their economic ideology, it gets repressed.

In late 2003 Labor leader Mark Latham broke the mould of studied ignorance when he accepted my invitation for a tour of the Styx Valley in 2004.

Forestry Tasmania has been exempted from Tasmania's Freedom of Information Act, so that public inquiry into its activities is stymied. At the federal level, millions of dollars have gone from logging corporations to the big political parties. On 21 December 1994, the very day on which the basis for the RFA slaughter was finally agreed to by the Keating Labor government, and endorsed by the Liberal opposition, three woodchip companies made combined donations of $242 500 to both parties.

Meanwhile extensive plantations of Tasmanian blue gums (*Eucalyptus globulus*, the state's floral emblem) have been planted overseas – an area the size of Tasmania in South America alone. These plantations are maturing and ready for the world's paper mills. Their wood fibre is cheaper and of better quality than that from our native forests, and could glut the world market within five years.

As export woodchip prices are falling, Jim Bacon's government and the woodchip corporations are looking to forest furnaces as an alternative. Forestry Tasmania's first furnace is on the drawing board as part of the Southwood project at Judbury, south of Hobart. It will burn 300 000 tonnes of so-called 'forest waste' each year in order to produce 30 megawatts of electricity (enough to light and heat a community of 60 000 people), which will be sold via the Bass Strait cable (Basslink) to the people of Melbourne as 'renewable' or 'green' power. The 'waste' is often the tree trunks themselves. When woodchipping began in Tasmania in 1970, it was going to use only 'waste' from sawmilling; now it consumes nine-tenths of the forests! Unsuspecting Melburnians, paying a premium for this 'renewable' energy, may end up burning possum nests with their morning toast. This deceit has been made possible by the passing of the deceptively titled Renewable Energy (Electricity) Act 2000, a federal act supported by both the Liberal and Labor parties.

The Styx Valley is only one site in Tasmania's forest holocaust. From the Tarkine Wilderness in the northwest, along the Great Western Tiers and across the Central Plateau, then in a thin ribbon running south through the valleys of the Florentine and the Styx to those of the Huon, Weld, Picton and Russell rivers, trucks are carrying millions of eucalypt and rainforest logs to woodchip mills. There are other areas being logged near the south coast and in the Northeast Highlands, including the beautiful Blue Tier, where trees have been dynamited to bring them down. Forests on the Tasman Peninsula and Bruny Island are also being felled.

This logging is a clinical process. First, Forestry Tasmania, under its managing director Evan Rolley, decides which areas are to be destroyed. All-weather gravel roads are built into the targeted area by Forestry Tasmania. Next, the chainsaws and bulldozers are moved in and every tree in the coupe is cut down. On steep slopes a cable-logger is employed: a huge iron pole is set up on the hill and wire hawsers radiate down the slope to winch the logs up. The best logs are trucked out, with more than nine out of ten destined for woodchipping. When the razed forest has dried out, a Forestry Tasmania helicopter drops hundreds of ping-pong balls filled with an incendiary which explodes on impact. The coupe goes up in a firestorm. No bird, insect, reptile, mollusc or marsupial survives.

Genetically selected, fast-growing eucalypts are then planted, either as seed dropped from the air or as seedlings. To ensure that animals from adjacent forests don't graze on the seedlings, blue-dyed 1080 poison is coated onto diced carrot and spread about. This poison causes an horrific and painful death, preceded by convulsions, loss of control of the sphincters – anal and urinal – and frothing at the mouth. Unlike on mainland Australia, where 1080 poison is aimed at feral pests, in Tasmania it kills native marsupials, including rare and endangered species. I have been told that 1080, which is tasteless, odourless and colourless, is banned from broadscale use in the United States, partly because of its potential abuse by terrorists.

The woodchip corporations plan to move in again in a few decades' time to cut these plantations. In this cycle the natural ecosystem is destroyed and its regeneration prevented, yet Tasmania's Deputy Premier Paul Lennon and Prime Minister Howard describe this clearfelling of native forests as 'ecologically sustainable'.

Driving the destruction of the Styx is the world's biggest hardwood woodchipping company, Gunns Pty Ltd. It has its head office in Launceston but exports its profits to shareholders throughout Australia and overseas. It is making huge profits from the once-only conversion of ancient forests to woodchips, and their replacement by plantations. The people of Tasmania own the forests and yet pay for the destruction of them – through massive subsidies, road upkeep and tax-breaks to the company, and through the cost of running Forestry Tasmania, which is largely an extension service facilitating Gunns.

Forestry Tasmania, the equivalent of the United States Forest Service, manages the public forests, raising money by charging a royalty, or stumpage fee, for each tree cut down by Gunns and other logging companies. Since 1988, more than half a billion dollars in subsidies has gone to Forestry Tasmania, half of it through the 1990 transfer by Michael Field's Labor government of $272 million of debt from Forestry Tasmania to the public debt, where, to be serviced, it drains money from schools, hospitals and police stations. When these subsidies are taken into account, Forestry Tasmania runs at a loss: the taxpayers are actually paying to have their forests chopped down.

Gunns is the conduit draining the forest wealth out of Tasmania. Its woodchip profits bounce to its share-holders outside Tasmania, including the Commonwealth Bank and Perpetual Trustees. John Gay, head of Gunns, takes an annual salary in excess of $600000 and has accrued millions more in other arrangements. His board members, including former Liberal Premier Robin Gray who ran the state into debt, are also rewarded very handsomely for their advice on how best to maximise the conversion of ancient forests to money.

They have a valuable backup, largely unknown to the public. Clause 8 of the Prime Minister's Regional Forests Agreement Act gives a compensatory guarantee in the form of 'resource security'. The purpose of this is to prevent the declaration of new national parks, thereby guaranteeing future access to public forests by logging companies, miners, and anyone else wanting to exploit the people's natural resources. (When Labor Premier Michael Field tried to introduce this in Tasmania in 1991 he lost government over it.) Acts creating national parks ensure that they are preserved for the people for all time. The Regional Forest Agreements Act ensures that forests are available for logging for all time.

Clause 8, an idea imported from the United States, was suggested by the logging industry's lawyers. It aims to guarantee that, should action to protect forests be taken by future federal governments, compensation will be paid. The God-given forests – for which the logging companies have not paid a cent – have been effectively transferred to the private domain of the logging companies. If Australians decide they want to protect their forests, they first have to pay the logging companies a bag of money – the amount the forests are worth as a pile of woodchips.

I fought every clause of this bill in one of the longest debates in Senate history. Yet the bill was supported by the Labor Party and ignored by the doyens of the press gallery. Throughout the debate, the government stolidly refused to give the Senate a definition of what John Howard defines as 'ecologically sustainable', because to do so would have put the lie to the highly unsustainable logging practices that he disguises with this term. The insistence that the destruction of the Styx Valley forests is ecologically sustainable is a bald-faced deception, typical of modern greenwash, which carries down from the prime-ministerial imprimatur to the hapless officers who put out the 1080-laced diced carrots to kill the marsupials.

The campaign to save the Styx Valley gained world-wide attention in 1999 when the Wilderness Society sent a team of intrepid climbers up an 80-metre giant that had been earmarked for logging. They put in place 3000 fairy lights, a dozen metre-wide baubles, and a giant neon star on top to create the world's tallest Christmas tree. It easily surpassed a 70-metre concrete tree in Massachusetts. The hidebound experts at the Guinness Book of Records spurned the idea of officially listing this Christmas tree as the world's tallest, on the grounds that it was a Southern Hemisphere eucalypt and not a pine! I wonder if they would also ban Australians from celebrating Christmas altogether, since it occurs down here in summer, with not a snowflake or a reindeer in sight.

The Christmas tree provoked Timber Communities Australia, promoters of woodchipping, clearfelling, fire-bombing and 1080 poisoning. Spokesman for the TCA, the ironically named Barry Chipman, who was suddenly concerned for the plight of the occupants of the forest, complained to the media that 'that tree at nighttime is now going to become daytime and that tree is the habitat for a lot of nocturnal animals and animals that their life is going to be disrupted by lights' (*sic*).

The campaign for the Styx is growing. Our grand Australian gardener Peter Cundall is a long-time advocate for Tasmania's forests. He has been joined by Planet Ark, who took singer Olivia Newton-John to see the giants and campaign for them. Actor Rachel Griffiths told a rally of 3000 protesters outside Hobart's casino that logging the Valley of the Giants was like quarrying the Sydney Opera House for pavement stones. Actor Jack Thompson, singers John Williamson, Jimmy Barnes and Paul Kelly, and authors Danielle Wood, Richard Flanagan, Peter Carey, Bob Ellis and Bryce Courtenay have all visited the valley and backed its protection.

The Styx has also been visited by the Catholic Archbishop of Hobart, Adrian Doyle, and the Buddhist Gyoto monks. In 2002 the Anglican, Uniting and Catholic churches held a liturgy for the forests, calling for their protection, followed by a rite of lament and confession. The politicians missed it.

They should not miss the splendid alternative plan for the Styx Valley: a proposal launched by the Wilderness

Society in February 2001 for a 15 000-hectare Valley of the Giants National Park. Like the proposal for the Gordon and Franklin Wild Rivers National Park twenty years earlier, this would see the Valley of the Giants become an extension of the Tasmanian Wilderness World Heritage Area. It would become as famous as Port Arthur, Cradle Mountain and the Franklin River, enhancing Tasmania's image and economy. It would be Australia's equivalent of the Redwood National Park in the United States.

Under creative planning for the park, damage which has already occurred through logging would be offset. The converted logging roads would carry hundreds of thousands of tourists, giving them roadside access to the big trees and wild scenery. Local towns which have been bypassed by woodchipping, such as Maydena, Westerway and New Norfolk, would see their shops, cafes and accommodation businesses expand.

Much of the southern side of the Styx Valley has been roaded and logged in the last half-century, and all of the biggest measured trees are south of the river. However, there are no roads on the north side, which has its own groves of giants – who knows that the biggest trees of all aren't there? When the Wilderness Society engaged consultants R.S. Graham and Associates to assess the possibilities for tourism in the Styx Valley, they found that it was unique, readily accessible, had in its *Eucalyptus regnans* the world's tallest flowering plant, and that it had enormous tourism potential. Their report noted that its 'giant trees are part of a living forest and cannot survive outside the broader forest environment. It is likely that the tall trees in protected remnants surrounded by logging will disappear in time.' The report concluded that, with minor upgrading of infrastructure (roads, parking places, walking tracks, viewing points and signage) and some basic promotion, there would be very rewarding economic outcomes for a Styx National Park.

Within five years there could be 20000 visitors per annum. This would generate an additional $1.5 million annually for the region and between thirty and 300 jobs. In the longer term there is potential for more than 100000 visitors a year, bringing an additional $8 million per annum and 150–500 new jobs. Compare this with the job-shedding, people-repulsive woodchip industry, which currently employs fewer than twenty full-time men in the valley, but which is endorsed by Liberal and Labor voters every time they enter a polling booth. The employment spin-off of the national-park proposal is in stark contrast to the gruelling and insecure contractual work of the remnant loggers.

Before I left the Tasmanian parliament in 1993, four log-truck owners came, in desperation, to see me. They were facing bankruptcy because a woodchip company had ended their verbal contracts. No Labor or Liberal politician would help. I advised them to park their trucks outside the doors of Parliament House, and they did – for weeks! This was to no avail, although one passing government minister was told by the men, 'Don't worry about us. Next election we're voting Greens.'

Even though the chainsaws are still eating into the giants of the Styx Valley, enough of its forests will remain for some years to constitute a truly great national park. The most potent weapon for blunting those chainsaws and ushering in the national park is public pressure on the politicians: in the ballot box, in their offices, through their letterboxes and across their phone lines. The 'urgent and consistent action' for forests which Australia, as a nation, promised the world at the 1992 Earth Summit in Rio de Janeiro has to come from the people. New Zealand and Thailand have ceased logging their prime native forests. Australians must achieve that logical goal too, just as we ceased whaling in 1978.

A list of what to do for Tasmania's grand forests is simple and has options for everyone. It is also a guide for action to protect threatened forests wherever they may be in Australia:

- Join the Wilderness Society, freecall 1800 030 641 or, from overseas, 61 3 6270 1701
- Shop at your nearest Wilderness Shop
- Make a donation to the Wilderness Society's Tasmanian Forests Campaign. Ask friends to do the same

- Visit the Styx, the Tarkine, Blue Tier, Huon and other forests. Camp out if you can
- If you have scientific, economic, fundraising or organisational expertise, please donate it
- Take photographs and get them published, or give them to the Wilderness Society
- Write to the national newspapers or magazines, or call talkback radio
- Write (handwritten letters are best) to Prime Minister John Howard or Opposition Leader Mark Latham at Parliament House, Canberra 2600, or to Premier Jim Bacon at Parliament House, Hobart 7000, or, most importantly, to your local member of federal parliament. Ask them what they will do to save the forests and whether they voted for the RFA bill
- Form your own local or workplace group to publicise or raise funds for Tasmania's forests. Book and art auctions do particularly well
- Do not bank or invest with Gunns' financial backers. Phone your bank and ask whether it invests, directly or indirectly, in Gunns
- Do not vote for candidates or parties that support the woodchipping of native forests anywhere, including the Styx.

And never underestimate the power of public protest.

Sunday 13 July 2003 was the day the Wilderness Society had bravely nominated for a mid-winter march in the Styx Valley to protest its logging. That morning, twenty or so campers on Gee Creek Road woke to find an inch of snow on the ground and on the great trees towering above them. This was cause for alarm: how many people would bother coming in such inclement weather?

A day earlier, logging contractor Les Walkden was reading the tea-leaves. 'I don't think the march will be well attended,' he told the Hobart *Mercury*. 'It's shocking weather out there.' But the ever-optimistic Wilderness Society still hoped for 500 to 1000 people.

As the march got going, writer Richard Flanagan told me he had woken that morning with a sense of despair. I knew the feeling. Why, with snow on the mountains, did we need to drive an hour and a half into the bush along muddy roads to protest something that most people opposed anyway? With both the Labor government in Hobart and the Liberal government in Canberra totally in the thrall of the logging companies, why bother? Hadn't woodchipping-corporation boss John Gay – dinner partner of Minister for Energy and Resources, Paul Lennon, the minister responsible for Tasmania's forests – just benefited from share options making him, on paper at least, $7 million richer in one day? How could patch-in-the-pants organisations like the Wilderness Society match the sheer public-relations spending power of Gunns, Forestry Tasmania, two governments and big business? Hadn't the corporations captured the law? Wouldn't people be feeling burnt-out, cowered, indifferent? Wouldn't they rather escape the demoralising prospect of forest destruction by staying home, snug and warm, with a glass of mulled wine and the Sunday papers? Why not have a leisurely lunch and risk no more than a walk with the dog in the park?

Then the Wilderness Society's Geoff Law got up on a pile of logs with a megaphone and told the crowd we had to wait: so great was the turnout that people had had to park kilometres back along the roads and walk to the meeting place.

The day became a triumph. Four thousand people turned up from all over Tasmania, creating the first-ever traffic jam in the Valley of the Giants. It was possibly the biggest public protest ever seen in the wilds of Australia. As the crowd grew, the mood of apprehension lifted. Showers gave way to sunbursts. Finally we all moved off behind a huge red banner which read, simply, 'Save the Styx'.

There had been a threat by loggers to bring out 300 counter-protesters, but this flopped. A few lyrical signs, painted in pink – 'Log the Styx', 'Shoot a Feral' – had been hammered into trees along the approach roads during the night, but these served only to raise the ardour of those coming to march for the forest and its wildlife.

In a newly buoyant mood, we walked six abreast over

a fast-flowing creek and up a steep hill. Our path wound through the giant trees, and as it rose, the snow-whitened tops of the Snowy Range came into view. Looking back set us gasping. The expected hundreds were indeed thousands. Red, yellow and blue raincoats coloured the throng. Yellow triangular 'Save the Forest' posters were sprinkled among the bigger banners, which read 'Save the Rainforests', 'Only 13% Left', 'Styx not Chips' and 'End Export Woodchips'. The road was peopled from hilltop to hilltop, sending our spirits soaring. This was a breakout!

As we walked uphill past the Chapel Tree – 83 metres high and with room for twenty-five people in its hollow base, a tree which would have already been cut down if not for the campaign by the Wilderness Society – we smiled and breathed in the arboreal oxygen, knowing that this turnout would ensure national media coverage and a new focus on the plight of the forests.

Back in town, the loggers were miserable. Paul Lennon called the protest 'a con, a farce and a sham'. With equal lyricism, Terry Edwards, CEO of the Forest Industries Association of Tasmania, branded the march 'a deception' and 'a fraud', claiming that the Wilderness Society had 'conned its followers into believing that the Styx is a pristine wilderness, has never been logged, and is the Valley of the Giants'. Timber Communities Australia's Barry Chipman complained weakly that the march was 'a protest for the sake of having a protest'.

Well, no, gentlemen. Those thousands of people have experienced the Valley of the Giants and taken it to their hearts. They will not now rest until it is free of your chainsaws, bulldozers and cable-logging machines ripping down the trees. That day in July 2003 was the day the Valley of the Giants heard the full roar from the hearts of people coming to save it.

In the spring of 2003 Greenpeace and the Wilderness Society set up the world's highest tree-sit: a platform 65 metres up the 83-metre tree known as Gandalf's Staff in the 'Lord of the Rings' coupe in the Valley of the Giants, which is due to be logged in 2004. As one of these bravehearts of wilderness preservation sat looking out over the rainforest, a wedgetail eagle soared past, almost close enough to touch, its feathers fanned out yet steady, its eye sharp, its confidence full, its future dependent upon the human spirit that put that platform aloft.

Another spirit was about to be lifted. In January 2004 Premier Jim Bacon was on board the new Sydney–Devonport passenger ferry *Spirit of Tasmania*, toasting its departure from the Sydney terminal. Four young men went over the side rails to unfurl a 30-metre red banner reading WOODCHIPPING THE. Pictures of the huge ferry with its port side now emblazoned WOODCHIPPING THE *SPIRIT OF TASMANIA* went around the world. The Premier was angry but millions were cheered. The day of the Styx being saved from the chainsaws had moved decidedly closer.

How Hyundai Will Decimate
a Little Aussie Traveller

One Hyundai company makes state-of-the-art cars. Another, Hyundai Engineering & Construction, makes sea dykes. This giant South Korean earth-shatterer has driven right over the top of public opinion in that country in order to build a 33-kilometre dyke which will enclose 40 000 hectares of the vast Saemangeum tidal flats on Korea's west coast, south of Seoul. Saemangeum is one of the world's great feeding grounds for migratory birds. It is to birds what Heathrow is to plane passengers – a hub of global importance – except that Saemangeum is to be obliterated, without warning the incoming traffic.

These mudflats have been built up over the ages from silt washing down the Mangyeong and Dongjin rivers. They border the shallow waters of the Yellow Sea, home to 158 species of fish, which is also enriched by silt from China's Yellow River and Yangtze River. The whole of the

Yellow Sea's land boundary is a shorebird rendezvous, and Saemangeum is the centre of attraction.

I visited Saemangeum with friend and bird expert Margaret Blakers in 2002. We stood by the shore, looking out over the mudflats to the horizon, as the tide came rushing in. The tidal waves move at up to 20 kilometres per hour, and the tides rise and fall by as much as 8 metres. I had heard about Saemangeum in San Francisco from 1995 Goldman Environmental Prize-winner Choi Yul, who set up the Korean Federation for Environmental Movement.

The KFEM, along with Green Korea United, and Wetlands and Birds Korea, is working with local opposition groups to save Saemangeum. The opposition includes women in big straw hats who wade almost knee-deep in the tidal flat's mud, gathering crabs and shellfish for the Korean and Japanese markets. A plastic tub skims over the mud behind them, hauled along by leather straps attached to their waists. The women carry ingenious seekers, made of wooden poles, which help sift the shells from the mud. Now their harvest is to be buried by Hyundai Engineering & Construction and the Korean government.

Ever since I made pre-dawn visits to the Coffs Harbour Fishermen's Co-op to help my father axe lumps of tuna from rotting carcasses with which to bait his lobster traps (in the 1960s, red-blooded tuna was unsaleable on the Sydney market), I've been averse to eating fish. But politeness compelled me to eat the shellfish and rice dish cooked by a happy woman in a shed next to the Saemangeum mudflats, and it was delicious. Her business is about to go too.

Other opponents of the scheme include eminent artists, scientists and religious leaders. Some of the latter have walked, bowing after each three paces, hundreds of kilometres from Seoul to Saemangeum in protest. There have been day and night sit-ins in front of South Korea's public buildings. A bicycle team has ridden around the nation for Saemangeum. Polls show that 83 per cent of South Koreans oppose the dyke project. Next to the group of sculptures on the shore are shrines to saving Saemangeum erected by Buddhists, Catholics, Protestants and animists. Besides the shellfish women, 22 000 local fishing people will lose their livelihood.

It is a worldwide phenomenon in this age of greenwash that governments never say they are behaving badly towards nature. In this vein, the South Korean government's handout on the environment ignores the Saemangeum dyke to talk in glowing terms about the value of tidal flats. South Korea's Wetlands Conservation Act states, rather wistfully, that the government has an 'obligation to save and preserve the tidal flats by all means'. The government is flouting this legislative stricture to proceed with the Saemangeum dyke and infill, which it calls 'environmentally friendly'. If the government says so, it must be so.

Hyundai Engineering & Construction has a marvellous pavilion, with flags flying, on a high hill overlooking its vast project. There are models, magnificent pictures of waterbirds and happy children playing in blue waters, and the company asserts that its project will enhance the environment. Below the pavilion, the southern arm of the dyke is being built straight out across the tidal flats. Trucks carrying rockfill trundle along the highway on the inside of the huge, two-tiered dyke (it is 200 metres wide and 30 metres high), and buses and cars scurry along the highway on top, taking sightseers to the moveable barrier near the end where red-uniformed young women with batons point to maps and pictures to help thrill visitors with the wonder of it all. The dyke is due for completion in 2004, and the whole 'development' by 2011.

Margaret and I were taken to the site by the effervescent Kim Choony of the KFEM, and I gave an impromptu talk outlining Hyundai Engineering & Construction's real environmental record to a busload of amused and cheering university students. Hyundai's dyke is more chilling than thrilling. When it is complete, it will be like a great bow enclosing the Saemangeum flats into which the two rivers flow, and these flats will be filled in to provide rice fields (although in 2001 the government introduced a new policy to cut rice production and so this need has gone), industrial sites and two freshwater lakes. The lakes will have none of the mudflats' ability to process the nutrients coming down the rivers and are likely to rapidly sour. Scientists have concluded that in due course the lakes will be polluted by organic discharge from cities and agricultural lands close by.

The dyke will be the world's biggest. To build it and provide the infill, more than a hundred mountains are being torn down. In a nearby national park, we were shown half of a forested mountain that had already been quarried. It stood forlornly decaying like a tooth with a giant cavity.

Each year hundreds of thousands of birds land from all directions to rest and feed on Saemangeum's abundant supply of worms, fish and shellfish. Some, like the little Mongolian (lesser sand) plover, fly west from Japan on their way to Siberia. Others fly from China, Tibet, Indonesia and Alaska. Australia and New Zealand have a lot at stake in Saemangeum. It is perhaps the richest tidal flat supporting the East Asian-Australasian bird migration path. Dozens of species of Australian birds fly north, via Korea, to Siberia to breed in the northern summer. One of these is a beautiful little speckled bird most curiously named the great knot, which has a long thin beak perfectly shaped to delve into tidal mud for worms.

We watched as flocks of countless great knots from Australia fed at dawn. As the tidal waves rolled in, thousands would rise together off the distant mudflats and land closer in to continue feeding. Through large telescopes on tripods we could pick out the detail of the delightful creatures. Soon they will not be there.

The great knots make an amazing flight from the tidal flats of northwest Australia, including those near Broome. They fly non-stop for three days and nights. At Saemangeum they gorge on the mudflat menu, recovering weight for the next, almost as long, flight to their nesting sites in Siberia. There they must mate, breed and raise their chicks within a few weeks, before the shortening days signal their return to Australia, via Saemangeum again, for the southern summer.

Hyundai Engineering & Construction's dyke will literally decimate this little Aussie traveller, reducing its global population by 30000, or 10 per cent. Altogether, some 350000 shorebirds come to ground at Saemangeum each year. Dozens of other bird species using Saemangeum will also be reduced in numbers, and for those already on the verge of extinction, this may be the finish.

Filmmaker Robert Lamb's compelling program on Saemangeum was shown in 2003 on BBC World's *Earth Report*. It featured the amazing spoonbill sandpiper, which Margaret and I also spotted as our telescope panned across the flocks of great knots at Saemangeum.

Ki Seop Lee, a Korean ornithologist who has been conducting a census of the visiting bird population, told *Earth Report* that his team had seen 200 spoonbill sandpipers at Saemangeum – that's 10 per cent of the total population of this rare bird. The completion of the dyke could cause their extinction.

During my visit to Saemangeum, I met with the extraordinarily polite and gracious South Korean Minister of the Environment, Madam Kim Myung-ja, and implored her to stop the project. The sweat ran down her brow as she wanly indicated that, while she wanted to, she had no power to do so. Appeals to President Kim Dae-jung, his attention diverted by the arrest of his two sons on corruption charges, went unanswered.

Back in Canberra I got a brisk response. John Howard's Minister for the Environment, David Kemp, approved of Hyundai's project, or at least had no intention of calling for its halt, even to protect Australia's birds. By late 2003, however, the public uproar had spread to Australia, and Minister Kemp let it be known that he had made representations about Saemangeum to Seoul.

Now South Korea has a new president, Roh Moo-hyun. I wrote to him in June 2003:

Dear Honorable Roh Moo-hyun
                                Warm congratula-
tions on your election as President of the Republic

of Korea. I very much enjoyed my visit to your country in May last year and look forward to continuing to learn more of its history, culture and environment.

My visit coincided with the time when thousands of birds migrating from Australia were resting and feeding on the mudflats of Saemangeum, before flying on to breed in Siberia. I spent two days touring the area and was thrilled to see the great number and variety of birds, as well as to meet some of the local fisherfolk whose livelihood depends on the fish, crabs and other shellfish of this rich and beautiful area.

Yet this magnificent place and all its wildlife are threatened with destruction through being reclaimed for farmland and industrial land.

I am writing to ask if you will intervene to save the Saemangeum wetlands for the sake of the whole world. They are one of the Earth's great wildlife habitats, of World Heritage value, and should be protected for all future generations to enjoy. Australia has a special interest because many wading birds depend on Saemangeum and will be threatened with extinction if it is destroyed.

The dyke is partly built but it is not too late to save Saemangeum. I speak for many Australians and many more people round the world who would be overjoyed by your decision to protect it.

It would be a mecca for birds, a livelihood for the local community, and a global icon for a sustainable Republic of Korea.

The president declined to reply, but please feel free to use this letter as a basis for writing your own protest to President Roh Moo-hyun. His postal address is Presidential Office, 1 Sejongno, Jougno-gu, Seoul, South Korea, and his email contact is webmaster@cwd.go.kr. Writing to President Roh Moo-hyun – all the better if you have a Korean friend who can do it in Korean – will help encourage the local defenders of Saemangeum.

If you are considering purchasing a car, go right to the top: contact the chief executive officer of Hyundai in Australia (www.hyundai.com.au) and ask what he (it is a he, not a she) can do to save Saemangeum so that you can feel easy about buying a Hyundai. Do not be put off by the predictable reply that Hyundai Engineering & Construction (their symbol is a green triangle!) is separate from Hyundai Motors. Technically that may be so, because the Hyundai conglomerate, or *chaebol*, was dismantled by law after the Asian economic meltdown in the late 1990s, but the Hyundai offshoots are headed by the sons of the original founder.

You can find further information about Saemangeum on KFEM's website (www.kfem.or.kr/engkfem) or from Birds Australia (www.birdsaustralia.com.au). And you could give the KFEM workers a nice surprise by sending them an encouraging email at jangiy@kfem.or.kr – thank you!

The Saemangeum project will cost US$2.3 billion. It will use the environmental lands, seas and rights of the nation, for which Hyundai will pay nothing, and will make the company a tidy profit. And if Ki Seop Lee is right and the spoonbill sandpiper goes into extinction as a result, Hyundai will pay no penalty. Not a cent.

In July 2003 Prime Minister Howard took the great knot's flight route to Seoul for talks with President Roh Moo-hyun. Before he left, I wrote to remind him of Saemangeum and to ask him to meet the Korean environmentalists – and got a dismissive letter from Environment Minister David Kemp! I assume that Mr Howard was too engaged in the issue of rogue states and weapons of mass destruction to think about environmental rogues, their mass destruction, and the fate of Australia's birdlife.

Shortly after John Howard's return to Australia, Chung Mong-hun, the most celebrated of the six sons of the founder of the Hyundai conglomerate, dogged by a scandal involving money sent to North Korea, jumped from the Hyundai building to his death on a desolate pavement in Seoul. He left a note asking that his ashes be scattered over the forests of scenic Mt Kumgang in North Korea.

Late in 2003 the Seoul Administrative Court of Justice ordered a three-month suspension of all works on the Saemangeum project by granting 3540 local residents and environmentalists an injunction. The court recognised the urgent need to suspend the project in light of the massive environmental destruction which, it feared, would 'erupt'. But early in 2004 came the news that a higher court in Seoul had overruled the suspension, following an appeal by the Ministry of Agriculture. The court's decision was based on a technicality – on the fact that Choi Yul of KFEM, who was the main plaintiff in the original case, was not from the area directly affected by the dyke and so had no legal right to take part in the court action.

Behind the scenes, the Howard government is working on a Clayton's treaty with South Korea to protect migratory birds. The treaty will be elastic enough to allow Hyundai Engineering & Construction's devastation at Saemangeum to continue.

These days, when I think Hyundai, I think dead birds.

The Balance of Power: How the Greens Behave in Government

There is a thin green line around the world. More than seventy Greens parties are spread across the continents, from Mongolia to Mexico, and from Kenya to Scotland, with 500 elected members in national or provincial parliaments and thousands more in local governments. As the Greens grow stronger, our aim lifts from simply gaining a toehold in office to gaining the balance of power, and then vying for opposition or government.

Those who have most to gain from conservative Liberal or Labor governments are fond of predicting doom should the Greens gain power. As Machiavelli observed almost five centuries ago, if anyone challenges the ruling people, let them prepare to be crushed. The Greens can expect a tirade from conservative editorialists, opinion writers and big business, and of course from the old parties themselves. We have already been labelled on the front cover of the *Business Review Weekly* as 'the green menace'.

To the rich, powerful and self-invested, the Greens' philosophy of guaranteeing everyone's basic needs, of determined ecological guardianship and real democracy can be profoundly worrying: the bank must not be vulnerable to the ballot box. And for the big-party supremos, sharing their existing monopoly on power is not something they welcome. Once it happens, they will start behaving like a dog fitted with a new collar.

Greens' experience in sharing government varies around the world. In Australia, the only state where we have held the balance of power in a lower house is Tasmania, and that experience makes an interesting case study.

In the state election of 13 May 1989 the incumbent Liberal Party, under the leadership of Robin Gray, lost office, winning only seventeen of the 35 seats in the House of Assembly. The Labor Party, led by Michael Field, won thirteen seats, and the Green Independents – as we were known at the time, not yet being a formal party – won five. Neither of the bigger parties could form government without us.

I retained the central Hobart seat of Denison, which I'd first won in 1983, and Gerry Bates, an environmental lawyer, held onto his seat of Franklin, an outer-Hobart/ southern-rural electorate, with an increased vote. Gerry was a skilled orator, and a source of lively wit and humour during our days in parliament.

Wesley Vale near Devonport, on Tasmania's north coast, produced two new Greens members: Christine Milne in the seat of Lyons, and Di Hollister in Braddon. Both had grown up in Wesley Vale and become teachers before throwing themselves into the campaign to save the village and its rich, vegetable-growing farmlands from a proposed pulp mill. The mill – to be half owned by the Canadian logging company Noranda and half by the Tasmanian woodchip company North Broken Hill, since bought by Gunns – would have exuded chemical pollution through its chimney onto the Wesley Vale farmlands, and would have piped 13 tonnes of organochlorine waste each day into Bass Strait. Premier Gray was gung-ho for the mill, which he announced in 1987. Christine Milne, the 'Boadicea of the Bush', leading a combined group of farmers, fishermen and environmentalists, was even more gung-ho to save the farmlands. After protests by thousands of Tasmanians, and federal intervention in the form of stronger environmental regulations, the mill was shelved.

Lance Armstrong, a Uniting Church minister, won our fifth seat of Bass, centred on Launceston. Following the election, we five set about our commitment to 'keep a hand on the shoulder of government', and began negotiations with both the Liberal and Labor parties on a list of policies in order to decide which party we'd support into government. Then Robin Gray suddenly withdrew from the talks. One seat short of a majority, he opted instead for a post-election campaign, backed by the logging industry, to keep him in office. He concentrated on the spectre of political instability, a strategy which fell apart when media and logging magnate Edmund Rouse, Commander of the British Empire, was caught offering a bundle of cash to the Labor MP he thought most likely to cross the floor and so deliver government to Gray. The MP told the police and Edmund Rouse went to jail.

We spent many days in this political cauldron negotiating a written agreement with Michael Field's Labor Party, and the resulting Labor–Green Accord ushered in the most exciting and progressive period of government in post-war Tasmania. In return for a slate of commitments from Labor – a final concession was the end of subsidised liquor for ministers – the Greens guaranteed support for the minority Labor government, including passing its budget and supply bills and attending all parliamentary sittings. The latter was essential because, as a coalition, Labor and the Greens had just one vote more than Gray's Liberal opposition. We also promised not to support or abstain from any opposition motion of no confidence in the government.

Between 1989 and 1992 the Accord rewarded Tasmanians with the nation's best Freedom of

Information Act, bills for gay law reform and Aboriginal land rights (although these latter two were stymied by the conservative-run upper house, the Legislative Council), and the end of a proposed mill to process millions of tonnes of old-growth forests at Whale Point in the Huon Valley. New national parks were created on the east coast: the Douglas-Apsley National Park, with its rare plant species which had been threatened by logging, and the delightful Friendly Beaches, site of proposed sand mining, which became an extension of Freycinet National Park instead.

But perhaps the Accord's greatest legacy – to this age in which Tasmania proudly uses its wilderness brand to internationally market its beer, wine, water and tourism – comes from the huge extension of the Tasmanian World Heritage Wilderness. This area is now a major direct and indirect contributor to the state's economy, employment and wellbeing. In 1982, at the height of the Franklin River campaign, 765 000 hectares in the southwest were listed as World Heritage. In 1989, through the Accord, this was enlarged to 1 384 000 hectares, an increase of 80 per cent.

This great result came after very tough negotiations in which we Greens were driving against Labor's wishes. The logging and mining companies, as well as their supporters in government departments and key Labor ministries, opposed the protection of almost every acre of that wilderness, and I knew that for at least a decade to come we would be hard put to win any more protection for Tasmania's natural heritage. It was the electorate's powerful pro-Greens vote and Labor's dependence on us to hold government that gave us, albeit temporarily, the required wilderness-saving clout.

Day after day, and often late into the night, we argued, grilling the government's experts and consulting closely with fellow environmentalists. We encouraged the federal Minister for the Environment, Labor's Graham Richardson, to come to Tasmania and mediate. Finally, as the deadline for nominations for the 1989 Paris meeting of the World Heritage Committee grew near, an exasperated Premier Field announced the new listing.

While he held his press conference, we persisted through Richardson and Prime Minister Bob Hawke's office to have an additional 40 000 hectares of wilderness protected – at Macquarie Harbour, Kelly Basin, the Gordon River rainforest and Sophia Peak. The pristine eastern half of Macquarie Harbour, now famous for Strahan's World Heritage boat cruises, was saved from the imminent spread of fish farms and shore-based developments.

Because we Greens held our ground in those early days of the Accord, the magnificently rainforested Little Fisher Valley beneath snowy Mersey Bluff is not logged; the alpine Central Plateau, one of the world's finest wild-trout fisheries, has had its damaging remnant sheep flocks removed; and the stunning Aboriginal cave stencils in the Denison River Valley, once threatened with dams, are safe. We also secured the protection of the Truchanas Huon Pine Reserve, and the forests of Farmhouse Creek and the upper Picton Valley (although, sadly, not the East Picton, Styx or Tarkine). Great lengths of southern and western Tasmania's spectacular coastline are now safely out of reach of the roads and railways proposed by old-time politicians, and to top it all off, thousands of jobs have cascaded from Tasmania's fame as a wild and scenic island.

But there was a black hole for this coalition. Robin Gray had left a $100 million budget deficit, and as a result the new Labor government slashed spending. The Accord provision for an increase in education funding was reversed, amid public uproar. Each of us Greens was savaged at public meetings in our own electorates, but we stuck to our promise and voted for Field's cut-and-slash budget.

We visited the schools that the Deputy Premier and Minister for Education, Peter Patmore, had listed for closure, and it was apparent that they were important to their communities and warranted being kept open. As parliamentary sessions drew to a close in 1989, Christine Milne drafted a bill to guarantee the continued life of twenty-two of these schools, and we confronted the Labor Cabinet with the legislation. Patmore was astounded, all the more so when, with Robin Gray's support, the Greens' bill was passed by both houses of parliament.

In April 1991 Christine moved a motion of no-confidence in Minister Patmore because he had broken a major commitment to fund primary-school education. The motion was no threat to the government as a whole, but that did not stop a remarkable pantomime being played out. On 16 April, as we five Greens met before the parliamentary debate on the motion, Premier Field's two chief advisers appeared at our office with a letter signed by the Premier and addressed to the Governor. It called for the dissolving of the House of Assembly: unless Christine's motion was withdrawn, Premier Field was warning us, he would call an election that day.

We showed the advisers the door, but it was not the letter that was rushed to the Governor, it was Peter Patmore. He resigned as Education Minister and the no-confidence motion became superfluous.

This ability of the Greens to deal strongly with the government on issues as they arose, while still honouring the Accord, meant that schools, as well as forests, were protected across Tasmania. New Town High School, for example, in Hobart's inner north, listed to be closed by Labor, is today an essential and dynamic school with 820 students and a great reputation.

Once in office, Labor's commitment to gay and lesbian law reform, Aboriginal land rights and freedom of information (FOI) waned. In each case the government's ministers, frazzled by public opposition or by the bureaucracy, floundered. When Peter Patmore, who was still Attorney-General, procrastinated on FOI legislation despite his access to excellent advisers and drafting staff, I drew up our own bill with the help of advisors in Hobart and Melbourne. After a fine tripartite debate in the House of Assembly, it shot through the Legislative Council at night. It was the most comprehensive FOI act in Australia, reaching out to cover local government. (However, since the bill's enactment in 1991, successive governments have repealed the provisions that allowed public scrutiny of the key instrumentalities of Forestry Tasmania and Hydro Tasmania.)

Seven of the provisions of the Accord related to forestry, including the fateful Clause 9, which stipulated that the state's export woodchip quota could not exceed 2.889 million tonnes a year. We wanted export wood-chipping to be phased out altogether, but had to compromise and settle for preventing future increases.

In December 1990 I warned Michael Field not to exceed this limit, knowing that he and his Minister for Forests, David Llewellyn, under heavy pressure from the logging industry, were planning to do just that. Field was developing a bill on forest reform to provide 'resource security' for the woodchipping companies – that is, guaranteed access to log all of Tasmania's unprotected forests. The bill would remove the woodchip export quota, assure the loggers of access to more than a million hectares of native forests, and ensure there would be no more substantial national parks or inclusion of vital old-growth forests, like those in the Styx Valley and Tarkine Wilderness, in the World Heritage Area where they belonged.

A process was set up to find consensus between the loggers and environmental groups. The feeble David Llewellyn tried goading the latter into signing his pro-logging deal; he failed. Premier Field threatened to bring in his bill regardless, and all through 1991 the controversy raged. Labor's position had a curious twist: the same logging industry that was now getting Labor's devotion had two years earlier been doing all it could to put Robin Gray into office at Michael Field's expense. By now Edmund Rouse, who had had a major interest in the logging company Gunns, was working in the hothouse at Hayes Prison Farm. But because Labor had no other vision for Tasmania's future (most of the party had been apprentices to Premier 'Electric' Eric Reece, who flooded Lake Pedder and whose dream was to generate enough electricity to turn Tasmania into the industrialised 'Ruhr of the South'), the government was marooned. With the end of dam-building, it saw woodchipping as a pivot of state development.

The Greens did not agree. Our vision was of an island

celebrated the world over for its unique natural beauty, its scenic wilderness, its wildlife and healthy produce. Where Labor saw woodchips piled on the wharves, the Greens saw educative tourism, organic agriculture, and design-based manufacturing. We were scorned by our political opponents as 'basket weavers' and 'Huon pine condom makers'.

In Cabinet, the woodchippers prevailed. In September 1991 Michael Field handed us a copy of his Forest Reform Bill, which effectively transferred control of the forests from parliament to the woodchippers. It reneged on the Accord's crucial Clause 9: there was to be no limit on the export of Tasmania's old-growth forests as woodchips. We relabelled it the 'Forests Destruction Bill'.

The Premier and his Cabinet colleagues seemed to think that there was some point at which the Greens, having made a political statement, would abandon our core objectives. After having taken a stand on our concern for the forests, Labor's wishful thinking went, we would back down. They were mistaken.

At a highly charged press conference in Parliament House, where our supporters had brought in great vases of flowers, we announced our rejection of the bill. I made it clear that if the Premier introduced the bill and so broke our Accord, I would move a motion of no confidence and his government would fall. A huge political storm was about to break.

I knew that a large part of the public was confused by the technicalities of the Forest Reform Bill, and, with Geoff Law of the Wilderness Society, planned a statewide letterbox drop to explain why 'resource security' was so bad for Tasmania. At the other end of public opinion, some environmentalists wanted action sooner, and friends told me that if I didn't take a harder line on the legislation, my reputation would be destroyed. I held out: if we moved before the public understood, we would lose.

Throughout this turmoil I was sustained by the four other Greens. I loved working with them; we were such a diverse mix. At times the tension grew, but in the end we were always there together. We knew that the political process itself had to change. Caving in to Labor's ultimatum, which was in breach of both a key part of our election platform and the Accord, would have deprived us of legitimacy.

The Forest Reform Bill was due for its first reading at the end of October 1991. By then we had gone through it with the feisty brainpower of our staff experts, dissecting the document and creating our counter-argument. The bill was worse than we'd expected, with, for example, no assurances made for rare and endangered species in the areas to be logged.

It struck me that a leap of faith was required, so I suggested to Michael Field that we have a much longer, easier meeting wherein we would put aside the Forest

Reform Bill and talk about the future and its possibilities. We had several meetings, where I tried to persuade him to take the Greens into his Cabinet rather than making us the opposition. He told me that Christine and I 'scare us [Labor] shitless'. I think this was because, while his government took refuge in the past, we kept yanking it out and into a different, more exciting but as yet untested future.

We got nowhere on the issue of Cabinet representation. In a later discussion I again made it clear that if he persisted with the bill we'd counter with a no-confidence motion. In order to stave off this motion, Labor would not only need to renounce the bill, but also give the Greens a commitment not to reintroduce it, and not to call an election before the next budget (for 1992–3) that is, before we had completed a three-year term in office. In an election we'd face the prospect of a return of the Gray government, since the Liberals needed to pick up just one more seat. The Liberals wanted to bring down the government and so would support a Greens no-confidence motion, even though they vigorously supported the bill. We wanted the government to survive, with an assurance that the bill would be knocked out. The Premier made no such commitment.

On 16 October a public meeting to protest against the Forest Reform Bill overflowed Hobart's Town Hall. On 31 October the bill was introduced to the House of Assembly before a packed public gallery. After Minister for Forests Llewellyn and his Liberal counterpart had put their cases, I put the Greens' case. Here is an edited extract from Hansard:

> The reality is that if we in this rich, lucky quarter of the planet cannot make a stand for the 30 million other species we share this planet with, let alone our own species, then who can? The major parties are locked into a 1970s mentality; they cannot see a new direction for Tasmania. And where do they get their direction from? It comes from those major industries which want to maximise their profits by putting people out of work and by continuing to cut down those forests.
>
> Over the past forty years the monetary return to the people of Tasmania for the cutting down of huge areas of Tasmania's forests has been minus $450 million – that is the debt that has been accrued through the mismanagement and the wholesale stripping of our native forests in the interests of those big companies. Every year the Tasmanian people we sit here to represent are paying $45–50 million just to service that debt. So they have had the forests cut down, they have had jobs shaven off, and they are continuing to pay a debt which never should have occurred.
>
> What about the public interest in this? We have

a government and an opposition which are here to represent that interest, but the public is being locked out. In this discussion of public interest I will begin where we should begin: with the Aboriginal people of Tasmania. Who in this government or in this opposition asked the Aboriginal community what input they wanted in this process? Where is it? Of course it does not exist. As far as the public ownership of the forests is concerned, the public do not get a say. We are here today making the defiant stand that we will continue to make for the environment, for our economy, for employment and for the long-term interests of future generations who do not have a vote and who will look back aghast.

I ended by moving the no-confidence motion and pandemonium broke out. The public gallery, full of pro-forest people, broke into applause. Suddenly awakened, a baby cried boisterously. The Speaker threatened to have the gallery cleared. The bells rang. The vote was counted. The Liberals supported the motion and Premier Field lost the numbers to continue in government. The Speaker called a three-hour recess to allow the Premier to go to the Governor and have an election called. I went to Field's office and gave him an alternative: if Labor agreed, by statement to the parliament, to permanently withdraw the bill, the Greens would return confidence to the government.

Field agreed to my wording of the binding paragraph. Having dictated it to his secretary, I took it down the corridor to confer with my four colleagues. Christine, savvy as ever, didn't think it was binding enough and felt Field would renege. But we couldn't see where the loophole lay; we didn't know how to make the statement more watertight.

When Field returned to the House he read his statement, which included my key insertion: 'The government accepts that the Forest Reform Bill cannot be reintroduced and will not be passed during the life of the parliament which the government intends to extend to the end of the 1992–93 budgetary year.'

The gallery clapped and whooped. People hugged each other. We had won!

The Labor caucus members, relieved that they had survived, broke out the champagne and partied into the night. Next morning, the mood in the streets of Hobart was extraordinary. It was as though a war were over. People were jumping about, clapping and laughing. Salamanca Place was full of exuberance.

But was the war really over? The newspaper headlines ran riot – 'Greens, Field Foil Libs', 'Field Hangs on to Power', 'Greens' Amazing Triumph', 'Green Tail Wags Labor Dog' – and the editorials were full of fury. Up north in the woodchip capital, the Launceston *Examiner*, Edmund Rouse's former pride, was black. 'If ever the State needed proof of the scunginess of the political climate,' it declared, 'yesterday's events give unhappy proof.' Likening Michael Field to Neville Chamberlain, the editorial excoriated Labor and denounced its decision as 'not only swift but shatteringly shabby'. The government had been pushed around by 'the single-issue Greens'.

The following week's politics were complicated. The rich and powerful were in a crushing mood; Field was pulverised. Union representatives took the role of middlemen in an operation designed to force Field to break his commitment to parliament not to reintroduce the bill. Notable here was the part played by the Secretary of the Trades and Labor Council, Jim Bacon (the current Labor Premier of Tasmania). He acted as a go-between for Robin Gray and Michael Field in a process which, three months later, would see the Labor government fall.

If Field, an amiable character, had had the vision to see that the popular mood against destroying Tasmania's native forests was there to champion rather than to shortchange, he could have been a great, enduring leader of the state. But he, like Opposition Leader Gray, was the industry's servant: Field had phoned me just before bringing the bill into the House to say that giving the logging industry secured access to native forests was his long-held dream. He was of that mindset and nothing would change it.

Within days, editorialists who had so often railed against politicians for breaking their promises were calling on Field to break his: 'it would be selfless, even statesmanlike', proclaimed the *Advocate*. Just one week after giving his promise, Michael Field broke it. He brought back the Forest Reform Bill. He altered the title page of the bill to read 'The Public Land Administration and Forest Bill', and insisted that it was not, therefore, the same bill! Therein lay the 'loophole' we had not been able to foresee. There is no antidote to political perfidy.

Having broken the Labor–Green Accord and followed that backflip with a double-flip, Field now depended for survival on Robin Gray's Liberals. Gray promised not to support the Greens' inevitable no-confidence motions – but only for three months. Those same caucus members who had toasted their survival with champagne just days earlier joined this pact of political suicide. On 1 January 1992, before the three months' grace that Gray had offered was up, Michael Field went back to Governor Bennett, who called an election for 5 February.

In that election we Greens held all of our five seats. Labor lost three to the Liberals, who swept back into power with a two-seat majority and to the cheering of the loggers. Robin Gray had been ousted as Liberal leader in December and replaced by his deputy, Ray

Groom, who became Premier. At a loggers' picnic during the Farmhouse Creek blockade, Groom had hurled a scarecrow-style effigy of a green 17 metres to win the 'chuck-a-greenie' contest, beating the Secretary of the Trades and Labor Council (now Deputy Premier), Paul Lennon, by 2 metres. David Llewellyn was 3 metres further back. The local mayor, Jack Kyle, told the press at the picnic that 'greenies live in the bush like bloody rats. Offer the locals $10 a head and we'd soon clean them up.' Groom, whose prize was a stubby of beer, then brought in the most draconian laws against forest protesters Australia had ever seen.

I had had a tumultuous few years in the sociopolitical machinery, and I started thinking about spending more time at Liffey and in the wilderness.

And so I resigned. Christine took over as leader of the Greens, becoming the first woman to lead a parliamentary party in Tasmanian history; Peg Putt, Director of the Tasmanian Conservation Trust, won my seat of Denison in a countback; and I took three years out, before, regenerated, I was elected to the Senate in 1996. Christine's Greens held the balance of power with the Liberals from 1995 to 1998, and this conjunction brought in Australia's best gay and lesbian rights laws, a suite of magnificent new national parks, and a parliamentary apology to the stolen generations, with Tasmania's Aboriginal people present on the floor of the House.

At the end of this period, Jim Bacon, who was by then leading the Labor opposition, joined Liberal Premier Tony Rundle to pass legislation raising the vote needed to win seats in the House of Assembly from 12.5 per cent to 16.7 per cent. The aim was to get rid of the Greens, who usually polled 12–14 per cent. Their electoral manipulation nearly succeeded: in the 1998 state elections only Peg Putt survived. But Peg, a magnificent parliamentarian, rapidly became recognised as the new Bacon Labor government's most creditable opposition. In 2002 statewide support for the Greens shot up to 18 per cent and four members were elected. Besides Peg in the seat of Denison, Nick McKim won in Franklin, Kim Booth – a sawmiller – won in Bass, and Tim Morris won Lyons.

During my campaign for the 1996 Senate elections, I got to know a campaign organiser, Paul Thomas, and we've been happily together ever since. Paul has carpet-wool sheep grazing on his farm overlooking the ocean in southern Tasmania, as well as a shop in Hobart where he sells colourful, handmade Tibetan rugs. We are great companions.

Antarctica:
The Last Wild Continent

In April 1990 I was one of six inaugural winners of the Goldman Environmental Prize, awarded by the Goldman Environmental Foundation in San Francisco, where I learned that part of the prize involved going to the White House to meet President George Bush senior. The opportunity to make a plea for saving Antarctica was too good to miss.

In 1990 the world was deciding whether mining should be allowed in Antarctica, or whether the great white continent, with its land-based colonies of seals, penguins and albatrosses and its rich marine ecosystems, would be kept free of mineral waste and pollution. One thing was certain: any oil or gold rush south to Antarctica would make the rush north to Alaska a century earlier look puny by comparison.

It was impossible to walk up to the President in the rose garden without attracting his bodyguards' attention, and having to reach into my breast pocket while standing there added to the tension. I drew out the envelope and placed it in the President's hand. Mission accomplished.

We prize-winners had penned the letter the previous day, appealing to President Bush to take action to protect Antarctica as a world park. 'Antarctica is the last wild continent,' it read. 'It is a grand region of mountains, ice plateaux, glaciers, and, with its seas, is one of the Earth's great wildlife sanctuaries.' The letter, signed by all six of us, went on to recall President Theodore Roosevelt's actions a century ago to guarantee America's system of national parks, and pointed to the need for US support in ensuring that Antarctica's wild and pristine integrity was retained for future generations.

Concerned that the letter would be passed to an aide and ignored, I asked the President directly if he would act to save Antarctica; he said he would 'look into the matter'. We were quickly assembled for a photo and the President was gone.

As the technology to drill through the mile-thick Antarctic ice had not been developed in 1990, mining companies had not fully embarked upon lobbying Washington to open Antarctica for exploration. Much more powerful groups than us Goldman six – Greenpeace, the Worldwide Fund for Nature, Friends of the Earth, and the Sierra Club among them – were already lobbying President Bush in the other direction. More potent

The great violinist Yehudi Menuhin launching my book on the
Franklin River in Melbourne, 1979

ABOVE My first trip down the Franklin, 1976

OPPOSITE LEFT Atop remote Federation Peak, 1976, a mountain that remained unclimbed by Europeans until 1949

OPPOSITE RIGHT The devastation wrought by mining in Queensland's Mt Etna caves, 1988

LEFT With Bob and Hazel Hawke (wearing her 'No Dams' earrings) at a Melbourne rally for the Franklin, 1983

TOP Signing the Labor–Green Accord with Premier Michael Field in 1989. Gerry Bates (right) and Peter Patmore (far left) are looking on

ABOVE With my fellow Tasmanian Greens MPs at Liffey, 1993: (L to R) Di Hollister, Gerry Bates, Christine Milne, Lance Armstrong

ABOVE Being hauled away by loggers at Farmhouse Creek, 1987

BELOW Under arrest in the Tarkine rainforest, 1995

OPPOSITE TOP Protesting the logging of the Styx Valley in 2003 with (L TO R) Peter Cundall, Geoff Law, Richard Flanagan

OPPOSITE BOTTOM 'Ecologically sustainable' logging in the Styx, 2000

LEFT This magnificent *Eucalyptus regnans* in the Valley of the Giants is more than 90 metres tall

ABOVE What used to be the world's biggest hardwood tree, burnt to death by Forestry Tasmania in 2003

OPPOSITE My home at
Liffey, with Drys Bluff in
the background

TOP With my staffers
Ben Oquist and Margaret
Blakers, 1996

LEFT With the Dalai Lama,
1996

Some of my own photos:

ABOVE Eddystone Point, the Bay of Fires

BELOW Wallaby in the snow

OPPOSITE Meander Falls, in the Great Western Tiers, protected as a World Heritage Area

TOP With Kerry Nettle during the 2001 federal election campaign

ABOVE Replying, 'So do we!' to George Bush's 'I love free speech', Australian Parliament, 2003. Kerry is next to me, Michael Organ in front. The sergeant-at-arms (right) is asking us to leave

OPPOSITE With two generations of Presidents Bush. TOP At the White House with Bush Sr and fellow recipients of the 1990 Goldman Environmental Prize. Rhoda Goldman is in red, and the late Michael Werikhe of Kenya is second from the right. BOTTOM With Bush Jr after his speech in Canberra, 2003

TOP With rock band Magic Dirt in Hobart during the 2001 election campaign

ABOVE With Paul on his farm

still, other Antarctic Treaty nations, including New Zealand, France and Australia, were lobbying to protect Antarctica.

The Antarctic Treaty, a remarkable document in global diplomacy, was already in place. It had come out of the International Geophysical Year of 1957–58, which saw great scientific co-operation between countries. In a continuation of this spirit, the seven nations with territorial claims to Antarctica decided to put them aside for the sake of a treaty outlining the future research and management of the continent. For once – and at the height of the Cold War – a territorial dispute was resolved with goodwill rather than gunboats. On 1 December 1959 twelve nations signed the Antarctic Treaty, which covered the continent and its seas south of latitude 60°S. They were Argentina, Australia, Belgium, Britain, Chile, France, Japan, New Zealand, Norway, South Africa, the United States and Russia (the Soviet Union). Today there are forty-four signatories to the treaty, including Germany, Brazil, China and India.

A year after my encounter with President Bush, I gained an unexpected insight into Australia's role in seizing the moment for Antarctica. Following Paul Keating's first, unsuccessful attempt in June 1991 to replace Bob Hawke as prime minister, he sat for a while on the back bench. Believing that it was only a matter of time before he got the top job, I phoned him with an invitation to visit Tasmania's threatened tall forests. He did not take up the offer, but he did tell me, during a long conversation, how he had returned from a trip to Paris in 1988 with enthusiasm for French Prime Minister Michel Rocard's vision of protecting Antarctica. France was seeking an outright ban on mining activities on the ice continent. Keating succeeded in convincing Bob Hawke and the Cabinet of the wisdom of this plan, and Australia joined France and New Zealand in canvassing support around the world. The United States had not yet come on board, and its support was pivotal.

The breakthrough came on 4 October 1991 in Madrid, where the world agreed that Antarctica would be kept free of mining for fifty years at least. Known as the Madrid Protocol, the agreement, which came into force in 1998, extended the Antarctic Treaty to ensure that mining would not be allowed before 2048, and then only if two-thirds of the signatories agreed. New regulations covering the protection of wildlife and the disposal of waste and marine pollution were also agreed to, along with international monitoring of the vulnerable continent.

An article the following day in *The New York Times* noted that the agreement 'was hailed as historic by governments and environmental groups alike', and then quoted Steve Sawyer, Executive Director of Greenpeace International, as saying that vigilance was still called for in Antarctica. Sawyer claimed that scientific bases had at times been 'environmentally disastrous', with some of them simply being deserted intact, and that new threats were posed by an increase in both the demand for Antarctic fish and tourist numbers.

Five days later, on October 10, *The New York Times* followed up with an editorial revealing that President Bush had been under belated pressure from the oil corporations, and that the American delegation to Madrid had tried to enforce a clause allowing the unilateral withdrawal of the United States after the fifty years was up. The president was ultimately embarrassed into relenting, and the existing compromise on a two-thirds majority was reached. The editorial concluded by noting that the 'decision to invade Antarctica ought never to be made lightly or quickly. Under the new treaty, it won't be.'

Antarctica is the world's only continent with no indigenous human habitation. Being so remote, vast, cold and wild kept it safely beyond human endurance until barely a hundred years ago, although the icy oceans off its shores were plundered by whaling ships, including those that harpooned the world's biggest ever animal, the blue whale, to the point of near-extinction last century.

The whale slaughter was gruesome. The scene at the whaling station at Grytviken, in South Georgia, has been described as one of scarcely imaginable violence and stench. Every year from the 1930s to the 1960s, 40 000 whales were killed in Antarctic waters. It is estimated that altogether 1.5 million whales died for candlesticks, oil lamps and margarine. Fortunately the International Whaling Commission has ended the slaughter, at least for the most vulnerable species, including the Southern Right Whale which observers think is now increasing in number. Efforts to protect Antarctica's whale ecosystem led in 1982 to the Convention on the Conservation of Antarctic Marine Living Resources, which has its administrative office in Hobart.

Blue whales are the grandest animals of all time. They are up to 33 metres long and weigh 100–120 tonnes, which is equivalent to fifty elephants, 2000 people, or a brace of tyrannosaurus rexes. Their calves feed on rich, fatty milk from their mothers' nipples and put on more than 2 kilograms of weight per hour. The blue whales' spouts, as they breathe out through their blowholes, blast 6–12 metres into the air. They live in all the great oceans, feeding in the polar seas north and south, and breeding in the temperate seas, with occasional visits across the equator.

In the past, blue whale populations were at least 100 000, but perhaps only 3–4000 remain. After the massive twentieth-century slaughter by Australian, American and European whalers, there are maybe only 1000 left in the Southern Hemisphere. Blue whale meat still turns up on Japanese plates, even though there is now a worldwide ban on killing them. The species is very seriously threatened, not just by pirate Japanese profiteers, but by the potential impact of global warming on krill, their feedstock, and our dumping of lethal chemicals, such as dioxins, in their habitats. In modern, anti-whaling Australia, corporations seeking the oil and mineral wealth of the ocean bed are using seismic testing, permitted by state and federal governments. This involves undersea blasts thought to deter whales. Close up it could damage their hearing anatomy and navigating ability, perhaps leading them to become stranded and die.

The fate of one of the inhabitants of the warmer subarctic regions of the Northern Hemisphere provides a bleak reminder of how much worse things could have been for Antarctica. With the Industrial Revolution in full swing and the economies of nineteenth-century Europe booming, feather bedding and pillows were in huge demand. On the semicircle of islands running from Newfoundland to Scotland lived millions of flightless great auks, the Northern Hemisphere's version of penguins. By 1844, the rookeries of the great auk had been so comprehensively plundered for their heat-holding downy plumage that not one bird was left alive. Huge flocks of these large black-and-white birds were clubbed, thrown into cauldrons and plucked bare, their bodies left in rotting piles on the shore.

Not all of them died for eiderdowns. The food industry was there too, to procure the birds' eggs. Although these hunters were early eco-villains – in the service of everyone snuggling beneath great-auk doonas in London, Berlin and Oslo – they might not have comprehended that the great auk was being exterminated. Even if they had, they would have been so busy struggling to survive in the polluted, impoverished European cities of the day that they'd have lacked the time and know-how to address the problem. Our twenty-first century, on the other hand, has the means to eradicate human poverty; the gluttonous world we live in has to accept its responsibility for protecting the global environment, for we lack neither the time, the comprehension nor the know-how to do better.

While the great auk suffered for its proximity to the Industrial Revolution on both sides of the North Atlantic, the same technology and capital was extending down to the other end of the globe. Macquarie Island, 1500 kilometres south of Hobart, is a subantarctic outlier, so far off the course to Australia that no European saw it until 1810 when Captain Frederick Hasselborough arrived.

As on all newly discovered islands, competition for valuable seal skins was fierce, and by 1821 the fur seals had been almost exterminated. In the first three years after Hasselborough's arrival, 180000 were despatched for their fur. The larger elephant seals were pursued for their blubber, which was rendered down for oil. The Russian navigator Captain Fabian von Bellingshausen watched a man smash a sleeping elephant seal across its sensitive nose with 'a club four and a half feet long and two inches thick: the end was bell-shaped . . . bound with iron and studded with sharp nails . . . The sea elephant gave a loud and pitiful roar.' As late as 1919 thousands of penguins were being killed and thrown into digester vats every summer, under the licence of the Tasmanian government.

Macquarie Island's ecosystem was further devastated by the cats, rats, dogs and rabbits that were taken ashore and which hunted the flightless Macquarie Island parakeet to extinction. In 1933, after a spirited public campaign led by Antarctic explorer Sir Douglas Mawson, the island was declared a wildlife reserve. Not to be put off, a consortium of Hobart businessmen proposed a scheme to revive the sealing industry in 1959. It would create jobs, they claimed, and besides, like the Tasmanian rivers then being dammed, the seals were a valuable natural resource which should not be let run wasted to the sea. But their proposal aroused public outrage. Clive Samson, the English poet who had migrated to Hobart, recognised that the combined interests of government and business would prove too strong for the scheme's opponents, and in order to garner world opinion he wrote a plea to *The Times* in London. The letter and the local campaign were effective: the Tasmanian government recalled the ship and the seals were saved.

Despite its bloody history, Macquarie Island, along with its adjacent seas, is today one of the world's most important wildlife sanctuaries. In 1997, eight years after a Greens' initiative in the Tasmanian parliament, the island was finally given due recognition and listed as a World Heritage site. These days it is the centre of a marine reserve covering 5.8 million hectares and its only industry is tourism. Fur seals colonise the island, and 20 000 or so elephant-seal pups are born on the beaches every year. One penguin colony alone has more than a million birds.

Though I dream of their wild, windswept remoteness and those vast colonies of wildlife, I have never been to either Macquarie Island or Antarctica, although I once tried to visit the latter. In 1971, as a 26-year-old doctor freshly out of hospital training, I took a three-month job looking after a general practice in Wentworthville, in Sydney's western suburbs. No sooner had I agreed to this job than my application to work in Antarctica was also accepted. Sticking to my word, but out of my mind, I chose Wentworthville over Antarctica.

It turned out to be a blessing in disguise: within a few months I had taken a job in Tasmania. I have since made a personal pact not to go to Antarctica. I mean to cause no umbrage to the lucky adventurers who do visit that continent – after all, my pact followed a dill-brained decision not to go when the chance arose – but I have become aware of the inevitable impact that my walking, rafting and driving has had on the wilds of Tasmania. That is my quota. I don't go along with the theory that, as there are already huge numbers of people going to Antarctica (or any other fragile area), one more won't hurt. A little restraint from each of us, in our own way, can be an enduring gift to the Earth.

By the terms of the Antarctic Treaty, Antarctica belongs to no nation, is nuclear-free, and is a shared domain for scientific research and exploration rather than exploitation. But despite this, it faces relentlessly growing pressure from humanity. In a crowded world, our common curiosity is focusing on areas of remote and pristine beauty, and Antarctica has become *the* place to see. The continent is now only days away from southern cities by passenger liner, and hours away by plane. Big money is eyeing it off. In the summer of 1999–2000 a total of 14 623 tourists visited on ships. That was as many as in the whole of the 1980s. Seeking unique places to spend the turn of the millennium in 1999, some people skied to the South Pole. Others parachuted in. Tourism has bombshell potential for Antarctica's ecosystem.

My friend Louise Crossley, who has spent many a long, dark night as a base leader in the frozen south, has quite specific fears about the tread of coming feet.

Interviewed for the Tasmanian Greens' magazine, *Daily Planet*, in 1996, Louise outlined some of the good and bad aspects of Antarctic tourism:

> Visitors are educated about disturbance to penguin colonies and there is some awareness amongst passengers about this. But there is virtually no attention paid to what people are trampling all over. One hundred people walking through a fragile moss bed can do amazing damage – particularly by not terribly active passengers who stumble a bit on rough ground and kick up ground vegetation. These mosses have a life cycle of around 250 years. Penguins, on the other hand have a life cycle of around 20 years. Damage to vegetation, in terms of ability to recover, is therefore far more significant but it isn't an issue.
>
> Ten thousand people visited Antarctica this year and most of them go to the Peninsular region. I have seen the damage that 100 people can do. If you can imagine 100 times that damage the impact is simply mind boggling.

Louise contrasted the management of tourism on subantarctic Macquarie Island, over which Australia has sovereignty, with that in Antarctica. On the former, the number of visiting ships is regulated and there's a charge of $200 per person. This money pays for park rangers, walkways and viewing points, to limit disturbance to the ecosystem, and tourists may not walk anywhere but on the walkways. But on the Antarctic Peninsula and the offshore islands claimed by other countries:

> There is a kind of attitude amongst tourists and expedition leaders that it is fun to find a new place that tourist ships have not been before. So the damage is very widespread and growing fast.
>
> There are, of course, good reasons for highlighting the advantages of tourism over the old 'smokestack' industries. But we should make no mistake, personal travel is yet another form of consumption and it can create immense damage to natural resources.

Contrast that with our plans for tourism to save the Styx Valley! There's no doubt that, had mining gone ahead in Antarctica, we would see tourism as the better bet. It is the lesser of evils in wild places, but nevertheless requires strong, long-sighted management plans where it does proceed. Infrastructure within protected areas should be publicly owned and controlled.

Besides the two dozen bases already in the frozen south, there is newly mounting pressure to build coastal airstrips for use by jumbo jets. This would open the way for a wave of tourists in previously unvisited sites, all keen to get close to the wildlife. Antarctica and the subantarctic regions need the world's best practice when it comes to tourism, including enforced regulations to ensure that threats are minimised. Tourist numbers should be capped. At present, on top of the 20 000 or so tourists who are landing each year, another 5–10 000 are cruising through or flying over for a glimpse of ice with a glass of champagne. And the numbers are set to escalate.

But even the act of cruising past or flying overhead – with the accompanying bright lights or loud noise – can have serious consequences. South African scientists John Cooper, Nico Avenant and Peter Lafite pointed to the impact of aerial visitors on Antarctic wildlife in a 1994 paper in the journal *Polar Record*:

> Research on heart-beat rates of breeding Adélie penguins (*Pygoscelis adeliae*) has shown that rates increase as helicopters fly in the vicinity of their colonies . . . Closer approaches of aircraft can lead to mass panic and flight from nests, resulting in loss of eggs and chicks to breakages, chilling, and predation by scavenging birds . . . Local decreases of Antarctic penguin populations have been reported in the vicinity of stations, thought due to human disturbance, including that from aircraft flying in the vicinity of breeding colonies.

The Madrid Protocol subjects all human activity in Antarctica to environmental assessment, enforceable by the laws of the treaty's signatory nations. People who harass penguins can therefore face a jail term, or, when they get back to the US, for example, a $10000 fine. But no laws can obviate the potential for oil spills as the volume of shipping in Antarctic waters increases. Nor did the Madrid Protocol alter the French government's determination to build a $1 billion airstrip by flattening three rocky islands and filling the area in between with rubble, at Dumont D'Urville on the coast of Adélie Land in the early 1990s. The islands were the nesting grounds for hundreds of Adélie penguins. The noble promoters of the protocol had become the despoilers: no doubt the runway proponents in the French bureaucracy used terms like 'environmentally world-class' or 'ecologically sustainable'.

Greenpeace led global protests, and published photographs of the islands being dynamited after the penguins had been trucked out of the way. The fiercely territorial birds scrambled back onto mounds of rubble in hopeless attempts to find their nests. In January 1992 we Greens hung a huge banner reading 'NON!' off Hobart's Kangaroo Bluff, opposite the dock where the French supply ship L'Astrolabe, carrying more explosives, was refuelling for another voyage south. Two Tasmanian protesters, Zana Laws and Grant Maddock, stowed away on the ship until it was too far south to turn around, causing international embarrassment for the developers. But despite all this, the airstrip was completed.

And then, what direct protest could not achieve, Mother Nature did for herself. In the mid-winter darkness of January 1994 a wild storm hammered the newly completed runway, causing extensive damage. The walls of the hangar, which sat some 3 metres above the sea, were smashed by huge boulders rolled up in the waves. Paris gave up and the strip was decommissioned.

The pressure on Antarctic wildlife continues in other ways, particularly on fish and krill stocks. Krill, while individually tiny, have the largest biomass of any species on the planet, and in their springtime growth weigh five times as much as the total human population. But the rapid loss of their Antarctic sea-ice habitat due to global warming has greatly reduced stocks in recent decades. On top of this, a new krill-rush, largely to feed aquaculture – for fish to feed the world's human stomachs – is on the way. Human exploitation is robbing the Antarctic larder used by seals and whales. The current krill kill of 100 000 tonnes per annum could rise to as high as 5 million tonnes per annum. Without the enforcement of strict regulations, the Antarctic fisheries will be fished to collapse, as has happened elsewhere in the world.

The latest rush is for the Patagonian toothfish, which

is as succulent as it is ugly. Australian warships repeatedly catch pirates plundering the profitable fisheries in waters off the subantarctic Heard, McDonald and Macquarie islands. This fishery's lines can extend as far as 100 kilometres, with numerous secondaries running off them. Longlines have spurred the rapid decline of albatross numbers. These graceful flyers, who have the largest wingspan of any bird, are caught on the hooks as they seek the fish bait. All this for the sake of appeasing the palates of pan-seared Patagonian toothfish-lovers in New York, Tokyo and Seoul.

In spite of these longline killers, Antarctica today makes the smallest contribution of all the continents to society's collective appetite for flesh. What it provides in far greater measure is the wildness, wonder and natural splendour that feeds humanity's malnourished soul. To protect this great balm for our collective spirit, we will need to treat it with a respect unprecedented in modern human history. Most of us will have to enjoy it from afar.

The American writer Henry David Thoreau wrote that 'in wildness is the preservation of the world'. One hundred and fifty years on, his observation might logically be reformulated to read 'in Antarctica is the preservation of the world'.

It would complete the great example of world co-operation shown by the signing of the Antarctic Treaty if

Antarctica and its seas were, like Macquarie Island, to be given official World Heritage status. This vast wilderness would take the place of honour at the top of the World Heritage list.

Indigenous Australia

Wadjularbinna Nyularimma is an Aboriginal woman from Old Doomadgee in the Carpentaria country in northern Queensland. She has seen a lot of change as her people's world has been desecrated, their land mined to profit shareholders who will never see it, and their gods forced to bow down to the god of market fundamentalism. She is a spirited woman who understands danger.

In 1997 Wadjularbinna took Margaret Blakers and me into the bush one summer evening as the lowering sun lit her country in an orange glow. Flocks of cockatoos and galahs screeched as they settled into the trees after a day of foraging on the hot plains. On the savannah woodlands dotted with cathedral-like termite mounds, the shift began changing to the wallabies, dingos and owls of the night. Wadjularbinna pointed out a native plum tree, explaining that her mother had taught her to take only the fruit she could eat, and never to break the branches. 'When the tree gives you fruit, be careful, do not hurt it. When your mother gives you food, you do not break her finger. Do not break the branches of the tree.'

If only the chief executives of giant corporations who are breaking the planet could understand such a spirited ethos. Where is the line between breaking branches for food and breaking the planet for money? None has been drawn.

Wadjularbinna's town of Old Doomadgee has a new $4 million police station to keep at bay the lawlessness which has resulted from European culture overrunning the Ganggalida people's own spiritually rich culture. Yet when we were there, efforts to find a few thousand dollars for solar-powered showers at their bush camp, set up to get youngsters out of the turbulent town and into the regenerative bush, had drawn a blank.

Wadjularbinna has an indomitable spirit but a heart seared with pain at the way the world is running down. She was in Canberra during the debate on the Native Title Amendment legislation in 1998. This legislation, which arose out of a High Court ruling that a pastoral lease on Cape York did not extinguish the rights of the Wik people, was touted as giving Indigenous people more rights, but in fact it reduced their ownership where pastoral leases were in place. It left them with only the right to negotiate over such things as the spread of environmentally damaging cotton-growing, the logging of woodlands, tourism (always aimed at the most lush, waterside places), fencing and fishing. Where leaseholders are changing the land of the first Australians, the latter are allowed to talk about these changes, but not to say no to them.

Compare this with the situation of the Inuit people in Canada, which is decades ahead of Australia when it comes to returning rights, lands and laws to its indigenous people. The Inuit, once known as Eskimos, rule Canada's first self-governing indigenous territory, Nunavut, which lies to the far northwest of Ontario and comprises 2 million hectares, or one-fifth of the country's land surface. As in Australia, the takeover of Inuit land was comprehensive 'and destructive, with societies and cultures wrecked in a wave of invasive settlement. But the Canadian experience shows that it is still not too late for Australia to make amends.

There remain large regions in Cape York, Arnhem Land, the Kimberley, Torres Strait Islands and Central Australia where Indigenous law, lore and language remain vibrant and the Indigenous population predominates, offering a real prospect for Nunavut-style self-government. This should be put on the table now, even if it seems, as it did for the Inuit people thirty years ago, the stuff of dreams. Behind the petty theft and misbehaviours that lead to Indigenous Australians being jailed at thirteen times the rate of non-Indigenous people lie cultural breakdown and disempowerment. If your culture and laws are not respected, why respect those of the conqueror? Self-governance is a prescription for returning the power and pride of Indigenous people, which in turn would bolster respect for white law. While not a panacea, the creation of Indigenous territories within the Commonwealth of Australia should be a national priority.

The similarities between Nunavut and Australia's Indigenous heartland are obvious: both are vast, isolated, sparsely populated regions, rich in resources and tourism potential. They also face similar problems: a young workforce with high unemployment, low education levels, widespread poverty, high unemployment, and poor access to goods and services. But in total contrast to the attitudes of Australian authorities, Canadian government documents on Nunavut are full of optimism; they describe the Inuit as bringing a unique voice to discussions on Canada's future and their young population as the source of future leadership. In Australia the debate seems mired in pessimism, frustration and matters of crime and punishment.

Queensland University associate professor Peter Jull, who took a key role in the evolution of Nunavut's self-governance, observes that Canadians, who have in the past been 'quick to fear for national cohesion, have largely welcomed the self-governing Nunavut precisely because it brings the most isolated one-fifth of their country full equal political status. It is a triumph of federalism, not a threat to it.'

It's high time Australia caught up.

Traditionally, Aboriginal people live in a dynamic and sustained relationship with the land. A critical factor in this relationship is their respect for a spirit of existence in the mountains and rocks and reptiles, as well as in warm-blooded creatures like themselves. Everything is linked, interrelated, undivided, one. They have, over thousands of years, altered the continent's ecosystems and this, along with the heating and drying of Australia, led to the extinguishment of the megafauna, such as the cow-sized wombats, 3-metre-tall kangaroos, and the mainland thylacines (Tasmanian tigers). This was neither deliberate nor foreseeable in the way that extinctions are now. The survival of the megafauna, as an important food source, would have been in the first people's best interests.

The sometimes savage arrival of Christianity ploughed straight through Aboriginal culture's Earth-linked spirituality. It could not, or would not, understand it, even though Christian societies themselves had a long line of ancestors who were instilled with comparable beliefs about the natural world. But Indigenous leaders in Australia have not given up. In 2003 Wadjularbinna, together with Neville Williams of Canberra's Wiradjuri/Ngunnawal people, called on Prime Minister Howard (who did not reply) to come to the Aboriginal Tent Embassy to discuss their document 'One Continent Two Systems'. This document outlined the clash between Aboriginal and material cultures and the need for connection. Here is part of it:

> We the First Nations Peoples of the Aboriginal Tent Embassy wish to remind the Commonwealth Government and politicians of this immigrant nation of 215 years that this continent that is now known as Australia has its own System of Laws, title to Lands and a unique social structure that was given to the many diverse nations of this Land by the Great Spirit Creator.
>
> Our connected and balanced structure is made up of female and male skin groupings which exist in all nations, in their own languages, with their own songs, paintings and stories unique to each nation. This spiritual connection to Land and Creation is the foundation of every Nation across this Continent.
>
> This System needs to be upheld and respected for the good of all peoples and the Land. We have the duty to uphold and teach the Laws of this Land given to us by the Great Spirit Creator to future generations of all races living in this Land. This Spiritual System cannot be reconciled with your man made foreign

system. There has been so much damage and desecration to our system in the 215 years of illegal occupation of this Land, which must be healed. This evil must not be allowed to continue . . . We believe we are of the land, as said in the Christian bible: Genesis, Ch.2 v. 7, 'and the lord god formed man of the dust of the ground, and breathed into his nostrils the breath of life, and man became a living soul'. Whereas the government, mining companies and multinational businesses see the land as a commodity to be bought, sold and abused to uphold this foreign unsustainable economy of greed that is in direct conflict with our system.

What is more valuable, money or country? For people who live in a place, it is country. For those who want to exploit the place from afar, it is money. On both sides, there are those who can be converted and those who cannot. Bill Neidjie was one of the non-convertible. He was from Alawanydajawany, on the East Alligator River in the Northern Territory, and I met him in 1996 when I visited the site of a proposed new uranium mine at Jabiluka (which he pronounced 'Jabilookoo'). The mining company had offered millions of dollars in compensation to the Mirrar people (Bill Neidjie was from the neighbouring Bunitj people) for the opportunity to turn their pristine, incredibly beautiful little valley into an industrial mining site, with roads from end to end. The people turned the offer down. 'I am not worried about the money,' Bill Neidjie told me. 'I am worried about the country.'

Speaking in his non-native tongue of English, Bill Neidjie explained his bond with his country to author Keith Taylor when they sat together under a tree in 1982:

> I love it tree because he love me too,
> He watching me same as you.
> Tree, he working with your body, my body,
> He working with us.
> While you sleep, he working.
> Daylight, when you walking around, he work too.
> That tree, grass – that all like our father.
> Dirt,
> Earth,
> I sleep with this Earth.
> Grass – he just like your brother.
> [He's] In my blood, in my arm, this grass.
> This dirt – for us
> Because we'll be dead.
> We'll be going [to] this earth.

More than 200 years before that, on the coast of Cape York, Captain Cook had had the insight to recognise that the Europeans were somehow losing:

From what I have said of the natives of New Holland, they may appear to be the most wretched people upon Earth, but in reality they are far more happy than we Europeans; being wholly unacquainted not only with the superfluous but the necessary conveniences so much sought after in Europe, they are happy in not knowing the use of them. They live in Tranquillity which is not disturb'd by the Inequality of Condition: The earth and sea of their own accord furnishes them with all things necessary for life, they covet not Magnificent Houses, Household stuff etc., they live in a warm and fine Climate and enjoy a very wholesome Air, so that they have very little need of Clothing . . . In short they seem'd to set no Value upon any thing we gave them, nor would they ever part with any thing of their own for any one article we could offer them, this in my opinion argues that they think themselves provided with all the necessarys of Life and that they have no superfluities.

Much can be said about such a different human spirituality, or non-materialist mindset. The high priests of market fundamentalism in their marble-foyered temples called stock exchanges would dismiss Aboriginal indifference to goods as 'primitive'. Yet is not doing better with less essential for human progress on Earth in the twenty-first century? We do not have to live in the bush to find fulfilment. But we do have to leave the stock exchange. As Wadjularbinna's mother knew, we are made from the Earth and resonate with it, and our self-respect is tied to how we respect the Earth itself.

The Fragile Coast:
The Bay of Fires

Australians have always been drawn to the country's stunning coasts, but the rush by more and more people to live by the sea in recent years has meant that increasing pressure is being placed on vulnerable shorelines. The push to develop these areas risks the very things that attract us to them.

The northeast coast of Tasmania, with its beautiful Bay of Fires, is an example. This coast has no high-rises, just long rolling beaches and endlessly moving, white-laced waves. With its crystal-clear waters, it is all that the rest of the world's seashores once were. Yet even here an urgent interplay has begun between nature and the city. The developers are on their way.

In the summer of 2002–3 I spent a week walking in this area with my partner Paul Thomas. Fine-grained white beaches are interspersed with creeks draining from the western hills, and the granite boulders of the headlands are encrusted with orange and red lichen above their high-tide line. The dunes are covered in silver-green grasses, or thick, sand-gripping woodlands with candles of yellow-flowered banksias. Sheoak trees whisper in the breeze, as they did for tens of thousands of years for Tasmania's Aboriginal people, who reached the island's shores across a 150-kilometre landbridge from mainland Australia more than 30 000 years ago. Aboriginal legend talks of that arrival across the land.

The Bay of Fires was named in 1773 by French Commander Tobias Furneaux, who saw the fires of the Aborigines as he sailed along the coast. There is a debate raging at present, at times rancorously, about the fate of these people, and whether the dispossession and killing of the full-blooded Aborigines constitutes genocide. In the early 1830s, the 200 who remained of the original 5–7000 Indigenous people on mainland Tasmania were shipped north to Flinders Island and taught the Christian catechism. Their own gods and dances were banned.

When Captain Stokes of the *HMS Beagle* visited Flinders Island in 1842, he found only seventy-one Aborigines still alive. They were subsequently shipped to convict quarters at Oyster Cove, south of Hobart, and by 1876 all were dead. Among them was the beautiful wide-eyed child Mathinna, the adopted then abandoned daughter of Governor John Franklin and his wife Lady Jane. Mathinna was left prey to the itinerant sealers and alcohol. She died at Oyster Cove, drunken and destitute, at the age of twenty-one.

According to George Robinson, who had been paid by the colonial government to round up the Aborigines for the move to Flinders Island, Launceston in 1830 was stirred by 'great preparations to go against the blacks; with few exceptions they [the Launcestonians] were exterminators'. Robinson was a paternalistic Calvinist, sure of his own godliness while set on eradicating that of the Aborigines.

Tasmania's present-day Aboriginal community is descended largely from the women who were taken into slavery by the European sealers and settlers. Anyone who laments their tragic past – or that of any other Indigenous community – is described by Prime Minister Howard as engaging in 'black armband history'. But what responsibility is attributable if, without genocide being stated as the goal, the outcome is still genocide? And what of the current destruction of entire ecosystems by human actions? Is that ecocide? Or can such behaviour be excused because it has not been stated as a policy, or because no single firing of the gun or swipe of the chainsaw brings about that result?

In 1831 George Robinson wrote of scenes that had been described to him by witnesses along the coast to the north of the Bay of Fires:

[A]t every boat harbour along the whole line of the coast the bones of murdered aborigines are strewed over the face of the earth and bleaching in the sun. These blanch relics and the blood of the murdered victims call aloud for vengeance upon the miscreant whites who have been guilty of these dire tragedies. Several skulls have been found perforated with musket balls.

Now the shoreline the Aborigines reached so long ago is also threatened. It can withstand the coming of many walkers and swimmers over the years ahead, as it has over years gone by, but it will not be able to survive the bulldozers, bricks, asphalt and nightlights of all those who want a piece of its beauty for themselves. Or, more particularly, to make money from that beauty.

As we walked south from the lighthouse at Eddystone Point, the northern extremity of the Bay of Fires, the scene was much the same as it would have been 1000 years ago. Gulls, oystercatchers and terns lifted off the beach to complain, fly around us in an arc and settle on the beach again. The sea was clear emerald for 200 metres, out to where a line of darker water marked the great beds of kelp beneath. These underwater kelp forests are the oceanic equivalent of Tasmania's ancient inland forests.

There was no-one else to be seen. In a summer-dry

depression behind the dunes, I stooped to examine three sharp-edged rocks of white quartz, together with a large round black stone which had been smashed in half, who knows how long ago, to form a cutting edge for killing seals. The seals provided food and, in the winter months, body grease for warmth.

We crossed another beautiful little beach, stopped for a swim, and then moved on over the next headland of boulders. Suddenly the wildness and remoteness of the shoreline was subordinated by a building – the new Bay of Fires lodge. On a privately owned block of land that abuts Mt William National Park, on the highest hill overlooking the northern end of the bay, it presents a windowed front wall and a commanding upswept roof, whose message to those on the beach below is 'Kneel, approach slowly, this height is commandeered.'

The modest-sized lodge has won great acclaim for its architecture and 'ecotourism' attributes, and yet its architectural qualities are leeched from the natural surrounds, from the unspoilt beauty of the bay itself. Like the disruptive glass pyramid in front of the Louvre in Paris, it celebrates its own robbery of the neighbourhood.

There are much more intrusive 'ecotourism' projects, and, as with the Louvre's glass pyramid, I don't blame the architect, for whom it is a triumph. The problem begins with the planners and politicians who let such incursions happen, and the buck also stops with them. In a world with so little land left unmarred by human intrusion, 'ecotourism' infrastructure should be kept out of undeveloped country.

There are signs that if developers want to utterly transform Tasmania's coasts, as they are doing in New South Wales and Queensland, the government will welcome them. A real-estate boom is on. It threatens the land, its ecosystems and wildlife. Where once the blubber-hunters and sealers marauded Tasmania's coasts, leaving them strewn with the rotting corpses of harpooned whales, now it's the turn of the developers – and the duck shooters.

In 2003 Tasmania's Minister for the Environment, Bryan Green, was implored to intervene against duck shooters who were waiting in hides to blast the ducks arriving on the east coast, 90 kilometres south of the Bay of Fires at Moulting Lagoon. Because of the nationwide drought, all other states had banned duck shooting, but Minister Green, declaring himself to be a duck shooter with thirty years' experience, rejected pleas to save the ducks in Tasmania. The concept that ducks should be protected from other deadly pressures when drought had already diminished their numbers was not one for Minister Green. The idea of a closed season on Tasmania's unprotected natural coastline is not likely to win more favour from Mr Green's colleagues in government either.

Tasmania's relatively untouched coast is a signature

to its 'clean green' image. It provides a beautiful experience for those who walk its beaches and come away leaving nothing but footprints in the sand. It stands in stark contrast to the high-rise beaches of the Gold Coast, Miami or Rio, and is still free of the impact of tourists who visit places like Thailand's west-coast islands in such massive numbers.

I once hired an open longboat in Thailand and sailed over the Andaman Sea, the waters of which, also emerald-green, are so clear you can see many metres down to the coral and fish on the bottom. As we skimmed and bounced our way down the coast, past the high-rises of Phuket where cruise liners dock to allow passengers to hit the shops, what struck me most was the great array of plastic bottles bobbing on the sea.

Why do people put the tops back on these bottles before jettisoning them into the ocean, or into rivers that run to the ocean? Because it's the easiest way to get rid of the top as well as the bottle. A search of the label of the major bottle producer, Coca-Cola, reveals a tiny triangular symbol with the word 'Recycle' next to it. No 'please', 'thank you' or 'how's your mother?' Through a one-word injunction to consumers, Coke's job is done, its conscience cleared. Its executives do not have to lose a wink of sleep or take any further responsibility.

The Andaman float is not on the stock exchange, so why should Coca-Cola worry? Maybe Thailand's tourists take the command to recycle literally and, there being no local recycling facility, hurl their containers into the Andaman Sea in the hope they'll float back to the United States, where recycling facilities are available.

In the face of the devastation wrought by tourism to beaches around the world, from Fraser Island off the Queensland coast to New York's Fire Island and the Mediterranean, you might assume that Tasmania, being an island state, would have a comprehensive, long-term plan to protect what is one of the world's most pleasant and natural remaining coastlines. But the Tasmanian State Coastal Policy (1996) has as its central objective not preservation, but sustainable development. This is an ideal that, by the terms of the policy, quickly becomes mired in contradictions. Reflecting many others the world over, Tasmania's coastal policy defines sustainable development as, among other things, 'avoiding, remedying or mitigating any adverse effects on the environment'.

If you have economic development in mind – such as a petrochemical plant, for example – then thank goodness for the word 'mitigation'. You can go right ahead as long as the environmental damage is 'mitigated'. This is a policy that pays lip service to matters of principle which are ignored in practice. In the hands of a government with duck-shooting proclivities, it becomes a policy free-for-all.

One of the policy's paradoxes relates to shacks,

which are defined as dwellings 'used for recreational and other purposes on a temporary occupancy basis at intermittent periods throughout the year'. In fact, shacks are often illegally constructed huts or cottages, built by distant townfolk on prime public land beside the sea in the days when much of the coast was remote and disregarded by the government. With the shacks came weeds, foreshore erosion, rubbish and sewage pollution. A decade ago there was a move to save the now very accessible coastline by removing such shacks. That move collapsed under a welter of self-interest. Successive ministers backed off on the concept of coastal protection and resorted to privatising the shack areas – selling them off so that the natural values of the land are lost to the general public.

Tasmania's coastal policy also asserts that 'development on actively mobile landforms such as frontal dunes will not be permitted'. In spite of this, owners of shacks built within a few metres of the waterline at Ansons Bay, not far from the Bay of Fires lodge, have hacked down trees and shrubbery, accelerating the collapse of the shore into the lagoon. In this mess it seems no-one has considered where the legal liability will sit when the sea levels rise from global warming, storms hit, and shacks are washed away. The public loses the land but will be shouldered with the costs.

While the Tasmanian Coastal Policy pays lip service

to the protection of cultural values, stating that 'all Aboriginal sites and relics in the coastal zone are protected and will be identified and managed in consultation with Tasmanian Aboriginal people', this is far from what happens in practice. In 2002, along with community groups that included Aboriginal people, I objected to a proposal to build a motel on the sand dunes at Planter Beach, in the Southwest National Park. The land earmarked for the access road to this motel was the site of an Aboriginal midden, but the Resource Planning Development Commission was unimpressed with our protests and gave the resort the go-ahead. The contractor for the road told the commission that the midden could best be protected by building the road right over it and burying it out of harm's way!

If ever there was a country where the people should make a stand for their coastline because it remains comparatively intact, it is Australia. All states' coastal policies should make protection paramount, and should legislate to ensure:

- No further sale of or building on public coastal land or foreshore
- Protection of all remaining wetlands
- No subdivision or building approval on sand or lowlands within 1 kilometre of the sea, or outside existing town boundaries

- A well-financed attack on weeds in order to give native species the edge
- Zero sewage or stormwater pollution of the ocean and the waterways flowing into it
- A ban on developers damming up or pumping out coastal rivers
- The promotion of water tanks and water efficiency
- A comprehensive marine-park system which would protect 30 per cent of the oceans
- The prohibition of plastic bags on or near the sea. The lead here was taken by the little town of Coles Bay on Tasmania's east coast, which in 2003, with the help of Planet Ark, banned plastic bags and gave free calico shopping bags to all the locals
- Free access to the coastline for Indigenous people, who never ceded it to anyone else.

And, in Tasmania, a memorial to the last duck shot by Bryan Green.

Farmhouse Creek and
the Role of the Law

Despite its name, there is no farmhouse at Farmhouse Creek; I don't know how it came to be called that. Perhaps, a century ago, someone walking up the Picton River, into which the creek flows from the west, saw it as an ideal place for a future farm. Farmhouse Creek tumbles down off the wild, grassy plateau of Mt Bobs in southern Tasmania, through dwarf alpine rainforest and then through tall eucalypt forests. As in the Styx Valley further north, the eucalypts hug the river for its richer soil, and for the warmer air in the valley floor.

I first went to Farmhouse Creek in the early 1980s, when just a single track had been cut down to the creek from the end of the logging road. The Franklin River had been saved from damming and attention was now on the destruction of old-growth forests by the newly established woodchip-export industry. To environmentalists, Farmhouse Creek represented a line in the sand: no logging machines should be allowed to cross it and move south into the untouched forests of the upper Picton.

When I returned at the start of 1986, with a state election in the air, it was clear the loggers were planning to bridge the creek. Phillip Hoysted, from the Tasmanian Conservation Trust, and I tossed up the options. We faced the eternal dilemma: would a blockade win or lose public support? We put our faith in the public's concern for the forests and began planning. In the ensuing election campaign, I warned that both the major parties wanted the people's votes in the ballot box before the election and their trees in the woodchip mill after it. On Monday 10 February 1986, two days after the election that saw the return of Robin Gray's Liberal government, the machinery moved in and the trees north of Farmhouse Creek started coming down to make way for an approach road to the bridge site. It was as quick as that.

The Wilderness Society hastily advanced plans for the blockade. I was now a member of Tasmania's House of Assembly and no longer the society's director, but I went to its office most days for lunch and spent a great deal of time there. (In my broom-cupboard-sized office in Parliament House, the government had denied me all equipment except a phone.) As had happened for the Franklin blockade, the Wilderness Society organised non-violent action training and insisted that people be acquainted with agreed rules before going down to

Farmhouse Creek. Scouts went in to look for campsites, and a back way in and out of Farmhouse Creek was established through the rugged Hartz Mountains National Park, in case the road access was blocked. We set up radio communications, which required somebody sitting out on the snowy mountain-tops. Communication from the valley was otherwise impossible: we had to establish a radio beam from Farmhouse Creek to the Hartz Range, and from there to the coastal town of Cygnet, where people could ring out to Hobart.

We had courageous people in the nearby logging town of Geeveston who were prepared to host blockaders and to let us know when log trucks, police or machinery were moving in and out along the only road. It was decided that the best place for a camp was right in the way of the proposed bridge across Farmhouse Creek.

A wide cross-section of the community backed us. I have a strong recollection of ex-Hydro-Electric Commission engineer Ralph Hope-Johnstone standing sturdily in his coat and tie and polished shoes, in the mud, on the northern side of Farmhouse Creek. An old man by then, Ralph stood with his brolly in the rain for a whole day – in solidarity with the forests. He had loved Lake Pedder, had helped on the Franklin River campaign, and now he was down here, done up to the nines, standing with all the conservationists in the bush beside the flooding creek.

At the same time, logging started in the Lemonthyme Valley, just east of Cradle Mountain, 300 kilometres to the north. So we were working on two fronts. The Lemonthyme protest turned ugly when loggers beat up some of the demonstrators. There was no media present to act as either witness or an incentive to restraint. The police failed to arrest anyone after complaints about this violence.

One evening at the start of March 1986 I was walking with my friend Judy Richter (now Mahon) and ABC journalist Hugh McLean, who was covering the protest, on top of a hill above Farmhouse Creek. It was getting dark when a van of pro-logging vigilantes cruised past. We knew this spelled danger; people had been threatened already. One of the men in the van yelled out, 'Are youse Bob Brown?' I did not reply and we kept walking; they drove downhill about 50 metres before stopping. A man got out, walked around to the back of the van, opened it up and took out a gun. He fired two shots in our direction. McLean, who had been in the army, had a sensible warfare reaction: he dropped to the ground.

After we reported this shooting to the police, the men were arrested and subsequently fined a couple of hundred dollars – for shooting on a Sunday! If it had been environmentalists who'd had the guns, there would have been lengthy jail terms.

This shooting was preceded by a raid on our Farmhouse Creek camp by two busloads of vigilantes, logging workers who were brought in from Hobart by the company heads. The Wilderness Society's Hobart office had been warned by an anonymous phone call in the middle of the night that the camp was going to be raided the next morning. It would be a big raid, the caller said, and would involve people at the highest level.

Anonymous calls are a feature of campaigns like this. There are people who might appear to be on the other side but who are also concerned for the environment. They can't afford to lose their jobs; they have families and need the money, they've got home mortgages and local ties, but they still want to help. Out of the blue someone will offer information, and you just have to accept that it's true. This happened in the lead-up to the Franklin protest too. In July 1982 we got a call from a woman saying that the first bulldozers would be moving down towards the Franklin River valley on the following Tuesday. And next Tuesday they were.

In response to the Farmhouse Creek tip-off, we moved more protesters down to the camp overnight. I went too and, sure enough, in the morning the buses arrived. The loggers had their orange hardhats on, and some forty police showed up. The Wilderness Society had alerted the media, who arrived soon after dawn and set up cameras on the southern bank.

Two D9 bulldozers came clanking and banging down the hill. A group of us moved forward so that when the

D9s got to the northern bank they were confronted by between sixty and a hundred people in the creekbed. Like tanks, the bulldozers clattered over the steep bank into the rocky bed, where the water was very low. While we were busy with one D9, another was crossing 50 metres further upstream, and some of us went up to try to block it. There was a general mêlée.

Judy Richter jumped onto the front of the first machine – like that Chinese man who, three years later, stood in front of and then climbed onto the tank in Beijing after the Tiananmen Square massacre. She slowed it right down, and when it came to a halt in the creekbed a number of us got on or under it. I went under with Karen Conellan and Bill Kent. We were curled right up among the creekbed boulders and it couldn't move again without the possibility of killing us; because of the metal tracks on either side of the machine, the driver couldn't tell how much room he had. There was a stand-off while he awaited instructions.

Back at our camp on the southern bank, two young women were hanging onto a group of leatherwood trees. A couple of thugs got a chainsaw going and drove it between their legs, cutting off the trees as the women screamed and cried. They refused to back off, holding their arms around each other and the trees. I'll never forget their sheer bravery.

Just a few metres from these leatherwoods was a

70-metre eucalypt occupied by Alec Marr, a bricklayer and bulldozer-driver with abseiling expertise. He had appeared at the Wilderness Society some weeks beforehand, set a platform 20 metres up in the tree and had been there ever since. The men with the chainsaw started cutting into Alec's tree. The wind was roaring and the whole tree was twisting and bending. That was a frightening enough experience, never mind having people chainsawing the bottom of the tree as well.

The police were looking on with their arms folded. One of them told me that they'd been ordered to stand aside and not intervene. Geoff Pearsall, the Deputy Premier and Minister for Police, was to deny in parliament that he'd given these directions, but the Gray government knew the blockade was on and had ultimate responsibility for the police refusal to act to protect people's lives.

I got out from under the bulldozer and went over to the men who were cutting Alec's tree, making sure they knew he was up there and that they were about to kill him. They had great swagger, but the man in charge of the operation, one of the company heads, stopped the chainsaw. I got back under the bulldozer.

A posse of men came down to the creekbed, grabbed Bill and carted him out by his legs across the rocks. Then they seized Karen by her ankles and starting pulling. Her long hair had wrapped around one of the boulders and was caught. I was trying to untangle it and she was yelling in pain. When they finally dragged her out, they came underneath the bulldozer and hauled me out across the rocks as well, ripping open my shirt, breaking my glasses, kicking and punching as they went. Had the television cameras not been on the bank right behind us, we would have been badly beaten up.

This was not the first time I'd seen mob violence, and it wouldn't be the last. Worldwide, violence has been a hallmark of the logging industry's attitude to those who want public forests protected.

In the protest at Farmhouse Creek the Gray government was involved in breaking the law. Under orders, the police stood by and did nothing while the scions of logging families who had helped establish the woodchip industry in Tasmania went to Farmhouse Creek and took personal command of an operation in which people were assaulted. In a lawful democracy these men should have been charged, convicted and jailed.

The Wilderness Society complained about the vigilantes, and the police took statements from all of us, but not one charge was laid. Judy had the determination to pursue a civil action; she took her case to the courts, and finally to the full bench of the Supreme Court, which ruled that Anthony Risby, Managing Director of Risby Forest Industries, was guilty of instigating an assault – but imposed no penalty on him. In 1986 and 1987 more than a hundred peaceful protesters, including Senator Norm

Sanders, were, unlike Anthony Risby, taken in police vans to Hobart's holding cells to await bail.

Compare Anthony Risby's treatment with that meted out to Neil Smith, known as Hector the Protector, a peaceful protester who in 2003 received a $7000 fine for sitting up a tree and delaying a logging machine for twenty minutes at Mother Cummings Peak, near Deloraine in the Great Western Tiers of northern Tasmania. When he refused to pay the fine, reduced on appeal to $5000, he was jailed.

It was Victoria's Cain Labor government who, in the 1980s, led Australia in introducing draconian penalties for citizens peacefully protesting the logging of state forests. In 1993 Ray Groom's Liberal government in Tasmania upped the ante and legislated to penalise protesters with up to a year's jail or $20 000 in fines (these penalties were recently halved), plus any costs incurred by the woodchip companies due to delays. The penalties for standing in the way of a forest officer became stiffer than those for standing in the way of a child-protection officer; threatening the wellbeing of chainsaws had become more odious than threatening the wellbeing of children.

And what about the fate of Brenda Hean, churchwoman and campaigner for Lake Pedder, who, together with pilot Max Price, disappeared without trace in 1972 on a flight from Hobart to Canberra to protest against the flooding of the lake? Their deaths were preceded by anonymous telephone threats – 'How would you like to go for a swim, Mrs Hean?' – and on the night before their flight, the hangar housing their plane was broken into. An axe was used to break open the door, and it was later discovered that the safety beacon had been removed from the plane and hidden behind some fuel drums. Premier Eric Reece refused a judicial inquiry into Brenda Hean's disappearance.

For all its accompanying injustices, the campaign for Farmhouse Creek succeeded. It led to a stay on logging and ultimately to federal intervention, when Labor's Environment Minister Graham Richardson came down for a look. Under threat of High Court action, the Gray government agreed to negotiate.

Two years later, when we Greens won the balance of power in the Tasmanian parliament, the forests of the upper Picton Valley beyond Farmhouse Creek were permanently protected. They are now in the Southwest National Park and Tasmanian Wilderness World Heritage Area. Without that defiant stand by hundreds of protesters, the forests and their wildlife would by now be gone.

One of these days, with enough Greens in parliament, we'll have laws that say if you send busloads of vigilantes into such old-growth forests, or even just loggers with chainsaws and bulldozers, the police will detain you and put you behind bars. Currently the making of laws is influenced by the rich, for the rich, to protect not the Earth and its people, but profits and property. Breaking the law in order to protect monetary interests is considered a much less serious offence than breaking it to defend living ecosystems, wild beauty, or the rights of future generations.

Guns and Gelignite:
Violence Towards Greens

M t Etna is a little limestone outcrop by the highway north of Rockhampton, in Queensland. In
1988 I was asked by a group of speleologists (people who
explore or study caves) to help campaign against the mining of the limestone by the Central Queensland Cement
company. I was delighted to visit Bat Cleft from which,
at dusk, thousands of bats fly out to feed on insects in the
warm tropical air. The cleft also attracts large green frogs
and pythons that gorge on the bats.

Donning hardhats, we crawled into underground
vaults where dozens of stalactites, including thin straw
stalactites a metre long, hung from the roof. We soon
entered a chamber of horrors, where magnificent cave for-
mations lay shattered from mining explosions overhead.
A stalactite a metre thick and weighing tonnes had can-
noned from the roof into the floor. Central Queensland
Cement wanted to turn these limestone features into

concrete floors in Rockhampton. There were good alternative sources of limestone available, including accessible deposits south of Rockhampton, but the company had its mind set on Mt Etna. The mining was being fostered by Queensland's National Party government.

Some months later, the speleologists, in a desperate last stand, entered the caves on the northeast corner of the mountain where one of the world's largest and most endangered species of carnivorous bat, the ghost bat, had its southernmost nursery in Australia. Central Queensland Cement lowered sirens into the caves, piercing the cavers' eardrums. They were driven out, some with blood trickling from their ears. The company lowered explosives and blew the caves up.

The environmentalists sought an injunction to halt the destruction in Queensland's Supreme Court, where they came before Justice Demach. His Honour found that blasting bats to smithereens was not an infringement of the decades-old Queensland law against taking protected or endangered wildlife. It appeared that environmental rights did not rate highly in his court. The defenders of Mt Etna had to abandon further court action because they were unable to risk the costs.

In his book *Places Worth Keeping* (1993), Tim Bonyhady noted that the general manager of Central Queensland Cement had admitted that the limestone would not be needed for another ten years, but this did not deter the company from demolishing the cave of the ghost bats immediately, campaigning against its conservation with the familiar assertion that they were creating jobs. Well short of that ten years, the company closed down and left Rockhampton, dumping its workers and shrugging off the needlessly destroyed caves.

In the March 1993 federal election, the Greens' lead candidate in Tasmania for a Senate seat was my friend since schooldays, Judy Henderson. With the election just two days away, she looked a winner. Top of our policy agenda was an end to logging in Tasmania's old-growth forests.

Then came the newspaper headlines. 'Railway Bomb', bellowed the Burnie *Advocate*'s front page. 'Environment Group Linked', boomed its subhead. 'Explosives Under Rail Line in Green Protest', echoed the Hobart *Mercury*. The stories were accompanied by photos of detectives near the Black River railway bridge in northwest Tasmania, which was used by logging trains, carefully examining an old can, a plastic bag, and the chemicals ammonium nitrate and diesel, a mixture that the *Advocate* reported to be potentially volatile. The police were holding up for the cameras a hand-painted banner reading 'Earth First, Save the Tarkine'.

The 'railway bomb' was a set-up, aimed at damaging the Greens' popularity with voters before the election. In state parliament, Liberal Premier Groom lapped up the headlines: 'It is most regrettable that some more extreme elements of the conservation movement may be willing to use the threat of violence to pursue their cause.'

The bomb shock came just eight weeks after public anxiety had been primed by Detective-Sergeant Terence Walsh of the Victoria Police Counter-Terrorist Intelligence Section. He had flown to Launceston to confer with local police and loggers about ecosabotage expected in Tasmania's forests. According to Mr Bernard Saunders of the Tasmanian Logging Association, known 'eco-terrorists' were thought to be in the state. The Launceston *Examiner* headlined its story on the matter 'Police Briefed on Forest Terror'. The fear turned out to be as unfounded as the speculations that the 'railway bomb' was the work of environmentalists. Nevertheless it helped change the outcome of the election and deprive Judy Henderson of her seat in the Senate: she failed by less than 1 per cent of the vote.

By 2002, with the destruction of forests now ripping along at twice the rate of 1993, things had changed. Public opinion was building against woodchipping and it was a major issue in the state election. So when an anonymous caller claiming to represent 'Anarchists International' phoned the media to accept responsibility for $4 million worth of damage to logging machinery in the Southern Forests a few months earlier, the reaction was different. Again the call came just days before an election, but this time there was no 'bomb' to photograph and the story was spiked. Peg Putt's Greens doubled their vote, winning four seats in Tasmania's House of Assembly.

Terrorising ecologists is a worldwide practice. In 1988 Chico Mendes, the Brazilian rubber tapper, environmentalist and union leader who fought against the destruction of the Amazon jungle, was assassinated. In Mexico in 1999 Rodolfo Montiel Flores and Teodoro Cabrera Garcia, poor farmers who blockaded log trucks, were tortured and imprisoned. Along with three fellow Goldman Environmental Prize-winners, I visited their prison in 2000. We were refused entry to see them but managed a short call by mobile phone. The following year their attorney, Digna Ochoa, was shot dead in her Mexico City office and President Vicente Fox relented to worldwide pressure and freed the men.

In Columbia, former Greens party Senator Ingrid Betancourt and her campaign manager Clara Rojas remain captives of the Revolutionary Armed Forces of Columbia in a jungle hideaway. Determined to fight the corruption, poverty and violence stemming from decades of civil fighting, Ingrid declared herself a candidate for the May 2002 presidential election. In the run-up to the election, President Pastrana ended a truce with the insurgents and authorised the bombing of the city of San Vicente, which had an elected Greens mayor. When Ingrid's office received calls from terrified residents she drove to the nearby city of Florencia, where an army general agreed for her to be flown by helicopter to San Vicente.

In an extraordinary turn of events, President Pastrana, who had been a lifelong friend of Ingrid's family, commandeered the flight and it was made clear that Senator Betancourt would not be flown to San Vicente. Frustrated but no less determined, she arranged a truck to take her along the dangerous road to San Vicente and en route she and Clara were kidnapped. Later in 2002 I flew to Bogota to campaign for our missing Ingrid, but she and Clara remain imprisoned in the jungle.

The renowned zoologist Dian Fossey, who was an intrepid defender of mountain gorillas, was hacked to death in her hut in Rwanda in 1985. Since 1997, poachers and the civil war have killed many of the 600 or so remaining gorillas at her research site, as well as eighty-seven of the park rangers who were defending them. Also in 1985, the French government, offended by protests against its nuclear bomb tests in Mururoa Atoll near Tahiti in the South Pacific, sent secret-service agents to bomb the Greenpeace ship *Rainbow Warrior* in Auckland Harbour, killing Portuguese crew member Fernando Pereira.

Swiss national Bruno Manser disappeared in 2000 while trekking in the rainforests of Kalimantan, in the Indonesian-controlled region of Borneo, close to the border with Malaysian-controlled Sarawak. He is presumed murdered. Bruno helped bring to world attention the plight of the indigenous Penan people, who have for years been fighting against the Malaysian loggers marauding their rainforests. Many of the Penan had already been murdered, tortured, or had their lives shattered by loggers and the Malaysian authorities.

In 1990 I visited the Sarawak logging region, boating well up the Baram River before being warned off by a government official. Some local men boated down the river overnight to express their village's sorrow at my expulsion and told me that in the old days the official's head would have ended up in a pot! A week later, in Kuala Lumpur, the secret police scared students away from a talk I was to give on the Tasmanian environment, and when I went to see the Mahatir government's minister for forests, he scolded Australia for its treatment of its Indigenous people as a way of excusing his own behaviour. 'You Westerners want to put the Penan people on show as if they are a circus,' he taunted, while arrogantly asserting that he knew better than the Penan what was good for them. Somewhere in the Penan's rainforests are the clues to the fate of Bruno Manser.

In 1999 one of my fellow Goldman Environmental Prize-winners, the gentle Michael Werikhe of Kenya, died in hospital after being attacked by thugs outside his home as he was leaving for work. Michael had walked thousands of miles in Africa, Europe and North America to raise awareness and money for Africa's endangered black rhinoceros. At the time of his death he was engaged in a number of rhinoceros-conservation projects in eastern Africa. Michael's wife had died three years earlier and his two young daughters were left orphaned.

One of 1995's Goldman recipients was Ken Saro-Wiwa, the famous Nigerian poet who campaigned against the despoliation of his Ogoni people's homelands by the Shell oil company. Ken was sentenced to death on trumped-up charges after a military trial that was condemned as fraudulent around the world. When the protests to save Ken and his eight co-defendants went global – in Australia the Greens picketed service stations – a Shell executive flew from Melbourne to Hobart to try to convince me that Shell Australia had no connection with Shell in Nigeria. Shell is a multinational corporation and had extensive business arrangements with the Nigerian dictatorship. The protests were to no avail and Ken and the others were hanged in the month following their trial.

Rarely are the attacks which kill such campaigning ecologists sudden ones. In most cases they are subjected to threats days, months or years before their assassinations. They are, quite literally, terrorised. 'You can't reason with eco-freaks but you sure can scare them,' points out the anti-environmentalist Sahara Club's Rick

Sieman. And according to Ron Arnold, spokesman for America's self-styled Wise Use movement, 'We are out to kill the fuckers. We're simply trying to eliminate them. Our goal is to destroy environmentalism once and for all.' Wise Use is not an organisation but a PR concept born out of the campaign to log and mine wild areas in the USA.

At a more senior level, President Ronald Reagan's high-profile Secretary of the Interior, James Watt, had his own sentiments: 'If the troubles from environmentalists can't be solved in the jury box or at the ballot box, perhaps the cartridge box should be used.'

A more restrained approach was taken by Tasmanian David Bills, who is now a United Kingdom forests supremo. In 1993, as a director of Australia's National Association of Forest Industries, he wrote that 'if violence [to environmentalists] does emerge, before passing judgement we should take time to understand the perspective of somebody being driven to financial ruin'.

In 1995 Col Dorber, Executive Director of the New South Wales Forest Products Association, also called for discretion: 'If we have to have a fight, if we have to physically confront those people who have opposed us for so long, then so be it . . . use your commonsense and make sure it's not being filmed when you do it.'

In Australia, as in the United States, the corporate sector has called for national intelligence agencies to investigate environmental groups (but not logging companies). Unlike Australia, the United States has some fringe groups dedicated to destroying property in order to advance their aims. This opens the door for the industry advocates to go into overdrive. Appearing before the US Senate Subcommittee on Forests after the September 11 atrocities by Al Qaeda, Nick Nichols, company chairman and self-styled expert on 'attacks by eco-terrorists', called on Congress to chase down such people 'just the same as foreign terrorists'. 'Unfortunately,' he said, 'even as our nation is at war with Al Qaeda and other foreign terror groups, eco and animal rights terrorists in our country continue to wage war against America.'

It is a pity that Judi Bari, campaigner for the protection of California's redwood forests, was not still alive to testify as well. Along with fellow environmentalist Darryl Cherney, Bari was injured when a bomb exploded in her car in 1990, a case covered by Duncan Campbell and Oliver Burkeman in *The Guardian* on 12 June 2002. The pair were accused by the FBI of planting the bomb themselves, even though prior to this incident Bari had received death threats which she reported to the police. A local newspaper later received a letter from someone calling themselves 'the Lord's Avenger', giving a description of the bomb and claiming it was retribution for Bari's pro-abortion stance.

The prosecutors alleged the bomb was in Bari's car

because she intended to commit environmental sabotage with it, but they had no evidence to support the case and the charges were dropped. Darryl Cherney commented that he and Judi 'were the victims of terrorism, but because the FBI and the Oakland police disagreed with our place on the political spectrum, they accused us of bombing ourselves'.

Bari and Cherney subsequently took civil rights action against the FBI and police, claiming that the attempt on their lives had never been properly investigated. The defence made consistent attempts to have the case struck off and it wasn't until April 2002 that it finally went to court, by which time Bari had died of cancer. The jury found that they had been the victims of a frame-up and awarded damages of US$4.4 million.

I know a little of how Bari and Cherney must have felt that night the bomb went off. On a Sunday night in 1993 I'd left the Wilderness Society's camp deep in Tasmania's Southern Forests to keep watch on the bridge over the Picton River. The bridge was the setting-off point for people walking into our camp for a peaceful protest against the clearfelling of the East Picton forests, east across the river from Farmhouse Creek. In the 1970s this former national park had been given over to the woodchippers.

The previous night, a dozen stakes had been driven into the tyres of protesters' cars. Earlier in the week, pro-logging vigilantes had burnt a barricade we had built across the topmost logging road and wrecked a Forestry Commission (now Forestry Tasmania) bus behind it. A phone call from a local had warned us that we were to be raided again, so we asked for a police patrol, but it never came.

Along the track I heard distant gunshots. I crossed the bridge, with the dark waters of the Picton swirling 10 metres below, and found a hiding place in the cutting grass and boulders near the buttress. Three other protesters, who had heard the gunshots and thought I might be in trouble, came running up from the camp. Suddenly a bright white flash lit up the night and I glimpsed the astonishment on my companions' faces. The bang that followed echoed across the steep, forested valley. This gelignite explosion, near our rebuilt barricade on the top road, began the raid.

'They're coming again,' I said to the others, voicing our common fear. 'Run back down the track to the camp. Don't hide in the clearing, just keep running!' I was interrupted by the drum of an approaching motor. Headlights speared through the trees. My friends disappeared and I ran across the bridge and scrambled into the hide-out in the cutting grass.

The vigilantes' vehicle had a searchlight out a front window and gun barrels on the sides. It came to a stop where we had been standing and I could hear the whine of a hunting dog. Slowly the car came across the bridge towards me, pulling up 5 metres away. The searchlight lit up the forest and then held on the grass where I crouched. Heart thumping, I kept my head down and waited for a gunshot, or for the dog to be let loose. But the car moved on, turned around and went back across the bridge.

It stopped again and the men got out. The dog was whining excitedly in the car. One man took the searchlight and a gun and scanned beneath the bridge. 'No-one here!' he bellowed, and they headed off on foot along the track to our camp in the forest. I hoped my friends had kept running; if they were in the clearing, they were in trouble.

'Look what's here,' one of the men yelled.

My heart sank. I pictured someone cowering in the light. But instead of a scream, a gunshot burst the air, followed by the sound of smashing glass and metal. They'd found our two hidden cars.

Two more tremendous explosions lit up the night and boomed over the valley. Flames leapt out and I could see the rainforest canopy swirling around as a column of searing air, filled with sparks, forced its way up into the sky. The cars became infernos. After a twenty-minute eternity, the men drove back into the blackness from which they had emerged.

Some time later, I heard a soft whistle and my three friends appeared. We inspected the burning cars, whose tyres were still flaming. My rolled-up sleeping-bag smouldered red hot in one of the ruins. The whole camp came up then, including a teenager with his motorbike, which he had taken out of its hiding place. We stopped him riding to Geeveston, the nearest town, in case the men were still on the road. He left at dawn to tell the Wilderness Society and the police.

The police found no trace of the vigilantes. The official report implied that we might have blown up our cars to create publicity. It suggested that two of us had appeared to withhold the information necessary for an investigation to succeed.

After this terror attack, the cable loggers moved in to convert the East Picton forest to a pile of woodchips. Every leaf in the great forest where we camped has been exterminated. The giant black brushtail possum that visited us for feeds is dead. That beautiful, life-filled ecosystem has been murdered. At the time, Prime Minister Keating, who permitted the calamity, was scolding our South Pacific Island neighbours for allowing 'environmental pirates' into their forests.

Why did the Geeveston police not patrol that night, as we had asked them to? Why were the vigilantes never arrested?

Around the world, out of reach of TV cameras or accountable politicians, brave men and women daily defy real terror in order to save the Earth. The preservation of the planet depends on such good-hearted people taking direct action, without violence, to defend it against exploitation. Many have died. More will die, or face violence, or be left traumatised by the onrush of bulldozers. Yet through their bravery the Earth's living biosphere sometimes wins. Judy Bari's beloved redwood forest is now a national park, and the remaining caves in Queensland's Mt Etna are protected. The click of the boots of tourists clambering up to see the bats has long since replaced Central Queensland Cement's sirens and gelignite.

Up in Jabiluka, surrounded by the Kakadu World Heritage Area, a different kind of ecoterror has given way to celebration. In the 1990s the Australian and Northern Territory governments, ignoring the concerns of the Mirrar people who are the owners of the land, allowed mining company Energy Resources of Australia to move into the untouched, unroaded Jabiluka Valley to dig a huge sloping shaft for the extraction of uranium. The Mirrar were deeply troubled for this pristine valley and feared that the mining shaft would rile the great Boyweg (gecko) beneath it.

Over the years, 5000 people went to Jabiluka to join Mirrar clan leader Yvonne Margarula and Jacqui Katona in opposing the mine. Margarula was imprisoned for trespassing on her own land, and both women were awarded the 1999 Goldman Environmental Prize. The Mirrar people refused money offered by ERA: money could not buy off their alarm for the land.

When uranium prices fell and the Mirrar were able to exercise their legal right to deny permission for a road between the mine and the processing mill at the old Ranger mine 30 kilometres away, the mine was mothballed. Now ERA and its new parent company Rio Tinto have moved in to refill the huge shaft. In the Jabiluka Valley, where the brilliant light of electrical storms heralds the life-giving monsoons each summer, the Mirrars' torment is over and the Boyweg keeps its sleep.

Meanwhile, around the world, we Greens are keeping alive the flame of hope for Ingrid Betancourt and Clara Rojas.

Tiger Economies:
Costing the Earth

There is no substitute for strong laws to protect the nation's environmental resources – its soil, water, atmosphere and biodiversity. But as long as market fundamentalism rules, the interests of big business will dominate and environmental laws will be designed to make way for them. Until the Greens are in office to protect the public interest, we say that the market should be true to the principles it espouses and factor into its activities the dollar cost of the environmental resources it uses or abuses.

This should apply to the loss of wilderness and scenic value, wildlife and its habitats (such as marine and forest ecosystems), sunshine (ask anyone who lives in the shadow of a skyscraper), and fresh water (ask those downstream of dams, mines or clearfell forestry). The market credo of everything having a price, as well as the principle of user-pays, should be extended to polluters, spoilers, and those who help drive species to extinction.

The world's fast-disappearing natural amenity should not be sold – what's left of it should be protected. But so critical is the current environmental loss that urgent interim action needs to be taken to force the market to abide by its own fundamentals, an argument not easily dismissed by the marketeers. Making the market pay for the losses it causes would slam the brakes on the accelerating rate of destruction.

What a band of thylacines would be worth today is anyone's guess, but it would be tens or hundreds of millions of dollars. There is already a multimillion-dollar effort to resurrect the animal by patching together DNA remnants culled from long-pickled museum specimens. The thylacine, or Tasmanian tiger, was once in fact the Australian tiger and roamed the entire continent; paintings of it are found in Aboriginal art sites at Kakadu and Cape York. After the great marsupial lion *Thylacoleo* became extinct 10 000 years ago, the thylacine was the top predator in Australia's empire of marsupials. Then, about 3000 years ago, it too became extinct on the mainland, because of Aboriginal hunting and their introduction of a new competitor from Asia, the dingo.

The dingo came too late to reach Tasmania. Perhaps 6000 years before its arrival, the thawing of the last ice age had caused the bridge of land connecting the island to the mainland to be swamped by rising seas. The thylacine flourished in Tasmania up to the time of the British invasion. In 1888, because of the threat posed to livestock, the Tasmanian parliament placed a £1 bounty on its head, and within twenty years, more than 2000 of these great striped beasts were shot for the equivalent of $2 each. Far from valuing the unique creature, the government funded its extermination. On 7 September 1936 the last known thylacine died in the Hobart Zoo.

In 1972 I caught the ferry across Bass Strait to Tasmania and spent eight months helping Sydney University student Jeremy Griffith and Tasmanian farmer James Malley search for thylacines. We set up a research centre in Launceston and followed up on 200 sightings. In almost every case the evidence pointed to the animal being a wild dog, cat, wombat or other bush-dweller. There were many stories but no tigers.

Wherever you live in Australia, chances are that thylacines have hunted where your house now sits. It was not actually a cat, but a marsupial – a kind of converted kangaroo which evolved to fill the niche for a big carnivore on the marsupial-filled plains and forests of the continent. It had fangs, and twenty or so dark brown stripes across its back for camouflage. It developed a sense of smell second to no other animal on Earth. As the thylacine came down off its hind legs to become a four-legged hunter, similar in proportions to a thickset greyhound, its pouch turned around to open backwards so that it would not get caught in the scrub. In that pouch the female carried her one, two, three or four pups.

You might think that once the imminent extinction of such a magnificent animal became apparent, every effort would have been made to preserve it. Yet even in the 1980s – long after extinction was widely assumed – when a National Parks officer reported an early-morning sighting of a thylacine at the edge of the Tarkine Wilderness in northwest Tasmania, the logging industry continued to lay baits of 1080 to poison marsupials. Since then this poisoning program has penetrated further into the Tarkine, which adjoins Mawbanna and Waratah where thylacines were shot as late as 1931 and 1933 respectively.

You might also assume that other countries would react to Australia's loss by ensuring living room and protection for their own tigers. But, as usual, dollars rule. Three of the world's species of tigers are already extinct – the Balinese, Javan and Caspian tigers. The other six species all face extinction in the wild. The most endangered of them is also the greatest of them – the Siberian tiger, which could become extinct in our lifetime. It is threatened not just by the loss of its habitat, but by the price on its penis and bones, a price created by the conviction some men have that extending their diminishing erections warrants the species' destruction. Among the more recognisable contenders for logs from the Siberian forests in the 1990s were Hyundai and Mitsubishi. Besides making fast cars, they saw a potential profit to be made from flattening some of the world's most magnificent tracts of temperate forest, including tiger habitats. Fortunately, under a hail of local and international outrage, their plans were dropped.

If the value of the Siberian tiger – to all of humanity for all future time – had been established and Mitsubishi and Hyundai billed that amount in advance, the logging would never have been considered. As it is, the Siberian tiger survives on the brink of extinction. 'The forest industry is capable of bringing impressive profits to the national economy,' President Vladimir Putin told loggers in 2003. In 2004 only 26 per cent of Russia's forests remain, mainly in Siberia. In addition to logging, huge wildfires from mining operations have devastated the forests.

Some people, *Asiaweek* magazine once reported, believe that tigers, like old people, have no real value and should make way for the things that do: 'It's encouraging to be told by the emotion-fuelled zealots of Greenpeace . . . that new species become extinct every half-hour . . . twelve extinctions a day comes to a satisfying 438,000 a century. Now it is the tiger's turn to face its karma. Whatever people think, nature has written the tiger off. Let it go.'

All life on Earth is interwoven, and humans depend on countless other species for their survival. Our fellow creatures, the animals and plants of the Earth, supply us with food, fibres, oxygen, pharmaceuticals and awe. The old adage that variety is the spice of life holds particularly true for our fascination with nature's profusion of flocks, herds, forests, shoals and entwined ecosystems. The legislated extinction of the thylacine has left us all diminished in our experience of life. The few faded film clips showing the last animal padding hopelessly up and down in its cage at the Hobart Zoo are no substitute for coming across it as a live, roaming beast, or even for just knowing that it is there. Hence our enthralment with extinct species and our readiness to pay huge amounts of money on so-far fruitless efforts to recreate them.

As the world's species disappear, so the potential for human fulfilment is eroded. We are entertained by other things besides wild nature, of course, including ourselves and a dazzling array of technologies, but our minds are deeply bonded to the Earth's natural ecosystem, and as nature is deprived, so are we. That bond resonates in the experience of day dawning or night falling in one of the remnant tracts of the Earth's wilderness; in areas where the noise, glaring lights, traffic and land scars of modern society do not intrude, and where our senses can be immersed in nature's infinite moods and dimensions. It is an experience that is now out of reach for millions of the world's people.

Yet to the market fundamentalist, the priceless is

worthless. As the rapture of nature is priceless, so it is not worth a cracker. The logic of assigning the financial cost of extinctions to the processes that cause them, or the value of natural vistas to the processes that threaten them, is missing from the market-based political discourse. Current inventories of the world's resources, which are used to measure commodities for the stock exchange, ignore intangible values such as beauty, wildness, remoteness, pristineness, or even experiencing these vicariously through our television screens. The marketplace is deeply cynical about such values. (As Oscar Wilde observed, a cynic 'knows the price of everything and the value of nothing'.)

Peter Raven, director of the Missouri Botanical Garden in St Louis, is a globally respected authority on the state of the Earth's biodiversity. In his 2002 presidential address to the American Association for the Advancement of Science, he noted that for 65 million years the rate of extinction of species was more or less constant: roughly one in every million every year. Today that rate is closer to 1000 in every million every year. The loss of habitat, rather than bullets, is now the greatest killer. Going by the current level of destruction of habitat, Raven predicts that by the end of this century, two-thirds of the Earth's species will be gone.

It's time to put the case for the Earth's preservation in terms the marketeers can understand: money. According to a 1997 study published in *Nature* magazine, nature is worth something in the range of US$18–61 trillion every year. Five years after this study was done, nineteen scientists and economists – led by ecologist Andrew Balmford of Cambridge University and including Robert Costanza of the University of Maryland – assessed the human value of places remaining wild in nature, and then calculated the loss in value that would result if they were converted to human usages, such as farming. Their work was published in 2002 in *Science* magazine (www.sciencemag.org), under the heading 'Economic Reasons for Conserving Wild Nature'.

The scientists estimated that the conversion of natural lands around the world costs some US$250 billion a year, and for every year into the future. They considered why such widespread habitat loss is still happening, and provided three answers. First, a failure of information: there is no price tag on natural habitats and they are therefore simply taken for free. Second, the exploiters will not stop while governments let them trash the environment at no cost. Third, far from making environmental exploiters pay for the harm they cause, governments actually subsidise the exploitation.

The team of experts calculated that the total annual cost of government subsidies to industries that were deemed 'economically and ecologically perverse' – that is, irrational in economic terms – amounts to US$950–1950 billion, 'depending on whether the hidden subsidies of external costs are also factored in'. If these subsidies were to be removed, not only would the rate of habitat loss decrease, but governments would save money. They could then invest the money in sustainable industries.

As Robert Costanza said in a University of Maryland media release, 'Natural capital is going to be more valuable as it becomes more scarce. In many cases we have passed the point where development is worth more to us than conservation.' Many a national treasurer would be gobsmacked to learn that protecting nature is a better economic prospect than exploiting it.

At present, only 7.9 per cent of the Earth's land and 0.5 per cent of its oceans are reserved. According to the international team, to maintain wild nature in the future, these figures need to be increased to at least 15 per cent and 30 per cent respectively. The cost of managing such protected areas would be US$45 billion, but would require just 5 per cent of current subsidies to be redirected and would produce an annual good worth US$4400–5200 billion.

This proposal for protecting natural resources does not argue against development. As Costanza and his colleagues point out, development is vital, given that roughly 1.2 billion of the world's population currently subsist on less than US$1 a day. It is the way in which this development proceeds that is the critical issue, and at present it is not only proceeding in an economically unsustainable way, it is resulting in a vast and worsening disparity of incomes around the world.

The case for environmental protection is both an economic and a moral one. Just as the saving of the Franklin River proved to be an economic winner for Tasmania, the ending of logging in Queensland's wet-tropics Daintree rainforests has seen an unsustainable industry with an annual turnover of $13 million replaced with a sustainable tourism industry that brings in hundreds of millions annually. Even the Howard government has been moved to act, and has extended the no-fishing zones of the Great Barrier Reef marine park because commercial fishing's annual revenue of $120 million is no match for the revenue derived from reef-related tourism, which is to be measured in the billions.

Sweden is attempting to address the issue on a national scale. According to a report in *Green Futures* in December 2003, its budget proposal for 2004 aims to go one-third of the way towards a decade-long commitment to move the equivalent of more than A$5 billion in taxes away from economic goods to environmental improvement. A big slab of this involves lowering income taxes across the board while raising the tax on carbon-dioxide emissions for both industries and households. Tax breaks on environmental investments are on the drawing board too, and there is to be more spending on the protection of wildlife habitats.

These are still pretty blunt measures and well short of costing the long-term losses to a community when developers clobber a wetland or a foreshore. But expect the trend to environmental accounting to accelerate, and for indices of community wellbeing – including such social factors as job satisfaction and quality of childcare – rather than monetary wealth to become the measure of how governments are performing.

Back in 1989, Alexander Downer, now Minister for Foreign Affairs and then Minister for Housing and Small Business, made a very sensible statement – since renounced – at an ecopolitics conference in his hometown of Adelaide: 'Most of the subsidies transfer from developers to the broad community – the ordinary people – the environmental costs of growth. Growth policies must, instead, allocate the cost of environmental damage to the developer. If we do that, then we will get better growth and a cleaner, more beautiful environment.'

Exactly.

George W. Bush in Australia: Manners Before Human Rights

'You are so rude!' That was a typical response from angry MPs, callers and emailers immediately after Kerry Nettle and I interrupted George W. Bush's speech to the Australian parliament in October 2003.

Parliament had been recalled for joint sittings of both houses, to be addressed by President Bush and, on the following day, China's President Hu Jintao. Australians, including their elected MPs, learnt of this parliamentary recall from news sources in Washington – not those in Canberra. All senators were to go to the House of Representatives for the joint sittings, and before these could take place, a motion had to be passed by each chamber agreeing that the rules of the House of Representatives would apply.

We Greens, together with the Democrats, were opposed to the presidents of the two foreign powers giving their addresses in the House, which is a debating chamber for the elected representatives of the Australian people. The parliament's Great Hall is the appropriate place for speeches by foreign dignitaries, and our view was supported by the rules of parliament, the Standing Orders. This document has no provision for anyone other than elected representatives to speak in the House. The Liberal and Labor parties voted down our alternative suggestion.

I then moved that there be provision for an hour of questions and debate after each president's speech, but all the other parties rejected this. There was to be no input from Australia's parliamentarians, except for welcoming speeches by the Prime Minister and the Leader of the Opposition. With trade and money clogging their vision, it was a certainty that neither would raise the abuse of human rights and international law by both major powers, so we Greens had a dilemma. We respect democracy and the parliamentary system, but why should we, representatives of the Australian people, remain silent on issues vital to the nation?

We talked this dilemma over among ourselves and our staffers. I knew that if we spoke up during either president's speech, it would bring a storm of denunciation down upon us. But if we stayed silent, or simply refused to attend, then we would feel worse: both these options surrendered the obligation to speak out on behalf of those who could not. I thought of what the thousands of people deprived of their political, legal and religious rights in China's infamous jails, including those in Drapchi Prison in Lhasa, Tibet, would think of such acquiescence.

But first came the matter of two Australians, David Hicks and Mamdouh Habib, held for nearly two years without charge and without legal representation in Bush's prison for suspected Al Qaeda members at Guantanamo Bay in Cuba. Bush had already repatriated the two Americans who had been sent to Guantanamo, so why not the two Australians? Or, for that matter, the 600 or so people of other nationalities, to allow them to face the justice systems of their own countries? Detaining prisoners under such conditions breaks international law, including the Geneva Convention. Whatever the guilt of the detainees may or may not be, they are entitled to be tried in accordance with the law. Moreover President Bush was treating Australians as lesser human beings than Americans. Why should Australia bow down to that?

There were two options to the silence expected of us – symbolic action or spoken statement. At first we decided on symbolism; during Bush's speech we would wear a lapel card with photos of Hicks and Habib and a sprig of Australia's floral emblem, the golden wattle. For Hu Jintao we would wear a Tibetan flag on our lapels and a black armband on our right sleeves, symbolising the political and religious prisoners in Hu's jails.

I had been to similar speeches before, and knew the

feeling of fraudulence that seeps into the bones with statements like 'We are working with your great country of Australia' while basic rights are being denied to fellow human beings whose only crime is to advocate democracy. I knew all about failure of nerve too, having first experienced it at a packed lecture given by the famed Chinese writer and Mao propagandist Han Suyin in Launceston in 1975, during the time of the Cultural Revolution. In her lecture Han Suyin insulted the Tibetans, so when question time came I rose, knees shaking, to challenge her, but sat down meekly as she poured scorn on the people whose ancient temples Mao's thugs were ransacking. So as the Bush–Hu double act approached, my anticipated shame at saying nothing grew.

George Bush arrived in Canberra on Wednesday 22 October. That day I met with Kerry Nettle in her downtown Sydney office. Michael Organ, who had recently won the first seat for the Greens in the House of Representatives, joined us by phone from Wollongong. Our staff gathered round and we went through our plans. The general public was to be banned from the gallery on both days, but each parliamentarian had been allocated seats for guests. The Greens had three of the nearly 500 seats, and for Bush's speech we had assigned these to representatives of the Guantanamo internees – David Hicks' attorney Steven Kenny, and Mamdouh Habib's wife and 18-year-old son Ahmed. For Hu's speech the seats were to be taken by the Chinese democracy advocate Chin Jin from Sydney, and two Tibetans, Dhondup Phun Tsok and Tsering Deki Tshoko, from Canberra. We had announced these plans in Sydney three days earlier.

I told Kerry, Michael and our staffers that I was thinking of standing during Bush's speech and calling for the Australians at Guantanamo to be given the same treatment as the Americans and repatriated. With the Iraq war in mind, I would also call for Bush to respect international law. Kerry said she wanted to raise the proposed Australia–US free-trade agreement, which was being negotiated behind closed doors and was the top item, besides terrorism, on the Howard–Bush agenda in Canberra. The obvious problem with raising issues from the floor with President Hu would be his unfamiliarity with English, so we planned to hold up a large, colourful Tibetan flag. As the Communist Party boss of Tibet in the late 1980s, Hu would recognise it immediately.

I made it clear that if nerves got the better of us, it would be okay to stay seated: it would be a daunting scene.

After our meeting, I followed Father Brian Gore in an address to a rally of 5000 Sydneysiders protesting Bush's visit outside the Town Hall. At 7.30 p.m. I was at the Institute of Technology Sydney showing slides of trees, wildlife, and Forestry Tasmania's logging malpractices to a meeting organised by Tarkine rainforest campaigners and the Wilderness Society. With staffer Cate Weate from our Hobart office I headed for Canberra by car at 9.30, arriving at my motel in Queanbeyan just after midnight. The sky was humming with the distant sound of helicopters: George and Laura Bush were in town and settling down at the American embassy. A 50-kilometre no-go air zone was enforced – with the exception of the security choppers – so that they could get a good night's rest.

A week earlier, the ABC TV comedy show *CNNNN* had appealed to Australians to be quiet on the night the Bushes were in town in order to help them sleep. Bush, for his part, kept many Canberrans awake all night with those helicopters flying overhead.

Next morning at 7.30 a Commonwealth car was waiting for me and I drove to Parliament House to have coffee with Ben Oquist and discuss the day ahead. At 9.15 I joined Carmen Lawrence, Andrew Wilkie and others to speak to the 3000 people gathered in protest outside. In front of Parliament House, special officers bearing guns and clubs were lined up. Behind them a row of tall, thick bushes in terracotta pots had appeared: a Bush shield so that the protesters, who were kept well down the hill, could not see him, and vice versa. The crowd responded warmly to the suggestion that, instead of spending another US$86 billion on arms for Iraq, George Bush should use it to ensure that the world's children had clean water, food in their bellies and a school to attend.

When we returned to Parliament House a military band was in place in the marble-colonnaded foyer, to play for the Bush entourage. I went to Kerry's office and met Mrs Habib and her son. She had written a strong, gracious letter which Kerry planned to hand to Bush:

Dear Mr President

America is the country that leads the civilised world with its system of democracy and justice. It is well known for its defence of human rights all over the world. It is the country of liberty, freedom, justice and dignity. As you yourself have said, it is 'a country that values human life'.

My husband was arrested in Pakistan two years ago and is currently a prisoner at Guantanamo Bay. He has not been charged with any crime – not under American law, Australian law or any law. In his two years of imprisonment, I have not been able to speak with him. How are his rights being protected by the United States? It is beyond any understanding how he could have been caught up in all this. He is an innocent family man who only had the best interests of his family and children. The youngest, who has only just turned three, does not remember her father.

Mamdouh has never broken any law of the United States or of any country. He is a decent and loyal citizen of Australia, where he has lived for 19 years, and was in Pakistan on family business. In fact, his only crime was that he was in the wrong place at the wrong time. If the United States government considers that he is a threat to its security, then please inform us of his crime and press charges against him. If not, then please return him to his family and his country.

At 10.55 the bells rang and at 11.00 we were standing at our seats in the House of Representatives as George Bush entered and came down the aisle, passing 3 metres to our left. Kerry and I were wearing our lapel cards with the prisoners' photos and sprigs of wattle. Michael Organ, similarly adorned, was in his usual seat a row in front. Labor Senator Nick Bolkus, sitting to my right, leant over and said presciently, 'I've got a good seat, near to the action.' Laura Bush was in the gallery, along with US secret-service men with guns.

John Howard and Simon Crean gave their short welcoming speeches. The black-robed Speaker of the House, Neil Andrew of the Liberals, offered Bush the podium, which was adorned with the Australian coat of arms. After a few opening pleasantries, Bush offered his scrambled eulogy to Howard, in which he claimed that the term 'man of steel' was the Texan equivalent of the Australian 'fair dinkum'. Fair dinkum! Then came a long recounting of the invasion of Iraq and Saddam Hussein's weapons of mass destruction. My heart began pounding. Bush moved on to 'freedom' and 'democracy'. It was now or never. As if on autopilot I was on my feet.

'Mr Bush,' I said, 'this is Australia. Respect our nation.' The President stopped his speech. Pointing towards the Habibs and Steven Price on either side of the chamber, I continued, 'Return our Australians from Guantanamo Bay.' Objections from the assembled MPs were coming rapidly, especially from the government side opposite. I ended with, 'Respect the laws of the world and the world will respect you.'

I sat down, feeling strong and suddenly settled. Speaker Andrew ordered me to leave the chamber. I ignored him and the President resumed his speech. The good sergeant-at-arms appeared beside me and told me to go. I waved him away. 'The Speaker has ordered you to leave,' he persisted, to which I replied, 'No: please tell the Speaker to read the Standing Orders.' I knew full well that when push came to shove only a vote of senators could force a senator out of such a joint sitting. The sergeant persevered and I asked him again to go. He did. Meanwhile Ahmed Habib had risen in the gallery and called out, 'What about justice for my dad!' He was bustled out.

Bush moved on to Southeast Asian and South Pacific security. From my seat I called, 'But we are not a sheriff!'

referring to his public comment in Washington a week earlier that Australia was a sheriff like the United States. This image of us toting a gun from behind an American badge was so damaging to Australia's relations with our neighbours that even John Howard had had to disown it. Then Bush was talking about the free-trade agreement and suddenly Kerry was on her feet, calling on Bush not to bully Australia but to understand our concerns about the pensioners' pharmaceutical benefits scheme and the livelihoods of farmers. It was a brave interjection on behalf of a large slice of the Australian population whose interests were being negotiated out of public view.

The President halted again. The House erupted in a cacophony of disdain. Then came Bush's one non-scripted riposte, 'I love free speech.' The mood switched straight to applause. 'So do we!' I called out, opening my arms wide in agreement.

Soon the speech was over. John Howard led Bush away for a meet-and-greet among the ministers at the table, then back up the aisle. Kerry and I moved to the rear of the chamber, surrounded by angry government members using very unparliamentary language to us. Kerry tried to give Bush Mrs Habib's letter, but was held back – quite illegally – by the phalanx of MPs and an attendant tugging her coat. Bush and I shook hands – a double thumb-wrap handshake from him – and made eye contact. Mamdouh Habib and David Hicks were on my lapel. As the jostling stopped, and with Liberal Senator Ross Lightfoot's elbow still jabbing my chest, I asked again for the US to allow the Australians to return home to face justice. Bush gave a noncommittal reply about 'looking at it' – much like his father's reply to my question about Antarctica in the White House garden some thirteen years earlier – and was moved quickly along and out the door.

With the President gone it was time for the government's retribution. Tony Abbott, Howard's Leader of the House, moved – in contravention of the rules of the joint sitting – that Kerry and I be expelled. Without debate, Speaker Andrew put it to a vote. The ayes drowned the noes. Yet there were a good many noes, besides those from the Greens. I stood and called loudly for a division – a properly counted vote whereby, after the bells have rung for a period, members move to the right of the chamber for a yes, or to the left for a no, and their votes are recorded in Hansard. The Speaker ignored my call and closed the session.

Back in our office, the phones were in meltdown, and that afternoon there was a barrage from hostile radio talkshow hosts. I took them head on. As they complained about the Greens' bad manners I barrelled in on international law, human rights, the illegality of Guantanamo Bay, and the potential cost to Australians of the free-trade agreement. Kerry also took on the aggressive interviewers, as did a good many of their listeners. America's CNN network had smuggled a TV camera into the gallery and filmed our interjection, and soon we were being interviewed for news outlets around the world.

Remarkably, an interviewer from CNN in London was the first to ask what we had actually called out to President Bush. Our words were not recorded in Hansard.

That night another storm was brewing. President Hu's team had arrived in Canberra, seen our actions on the news and was horrified. In dictatorships, no-one gets out of line like that. By 9.30 Speaker Andrew, after consulting with Senate President Paul Calvert, another Liberal, was under direct pressure to control the Greens. He had already banned us from the following day's sitting by accepting Abbott's motion.

On the Friday morning, an hour before President Hu's scheduled speech, Speaker Andrew called in Michael Organ and told him that the Chinese government did not want his much-publicised display of the Tibetan flag and black armband to go ahead. Michael made it clear that he would be wearing both.

The reach of Beijing was also having an effect up in the gallery: Chinese security agents had stationed themselves at the table where guests were required to present their official cards before entry. (Speaker Andrew later revealed that he had asked Beijing to have these agents present at the gallery's entrance to vet the Greens' guests!) As our Tibetan guests approached, one of Hu's men pointed to them and their cards were confiscated; a call was made to Speaker Andrew's office and the two were removed from the gallery queue. Chin Jin was also escorted away. They were taken upstairs and placed in a viewing area behind glass doors, a facility generally used by school children, with no headphones through which to hear Hu's speech. Speaker Andrew made no effort to consult the Greens MPs whose guests he had expelled with the aid of foreign agents.

Australia's Minister for Foreign Affairs, Alexander Downer, later told the ABC that 'Obviously they [the Chinese] were very preoccupied with what Brown and Nettle had done the previous day. This had shaken the Chinese, there's no question of that . . . if Brown and Nettle had done to Hu what they did to Bush, then I think the implications for Australia could have been rather serious.'

For 'Australia', read 'trade'.

Tony Abbott told the Nine Network that foreign governments did not decide who was allowed into the public gallery, adding, 'Except on this particular occasion it was important for Australia to put its best face forward to the world and the President of China.' That 'best face' was the face of a Uriah Heep government backing down on what should have been a clear, strong defence of Australia's democratic rights. President Hu, rattling the prospect of trade deals, cowed John Howard; the dictatorship had the democracy back down.

In the late 1980s Hu Jintao was the Communist Party Secretary of Tibet. He was there when forty civilians were shot down for demonstrating for a free Tibet. Thousands more, mainly Buddhist monks and nuns, were jailed and many were tortured. Hundreds still remain imprisoned, as do dozens of the gallant students who defied Hu's party in demanding liberty and democracy in Tiananmen Square in 1989. I would have spoken up to Hu if I had not been barred from the chamber, but when three burly men, acting on the Speaker's orders, blocked Kerry and me from the joint sitting, it was left to Michael to convey the message. He sat while the parliament rose to honour the President. After his speech, Hu came within a few metres of Michael and, looking directly at him, saw the Tibetan flag on his lapel and the black armband. The message got through.

Outside, we caught up with our white-faced Tibetan and Chinese guests. They were shocked by their expulsion from the public gallery at the behest of Chinese agents. They had had no intention of protesting. I assured them that while they might feel dismayed, in fact this would rebound. And so it did. The revelations about these behind-the-scene manoeuvres made news throughout Asia, and the cause of freedom in China and Tibet was highlighted far more than it would have been had these good people been allowed to take their allocated seats.

Outside 'the bubble' on Capital Hill, the mood was very different. In Hobart the next morning, I walked with Christine Milne into the packed Retro Cafe and the place broke out in applause. In the Saturday markets of Salamanca Place, people came up from everywhere and the most frequent call was 'Thank you, Bob and Kerry, you stood up for me!' In the following weeks, all around Australia, at airports, in shops and in the street, the response was the same: 'Good on you for standing up to Bush!' Thousands of emails and letters poured in, at first 70:30 our way but soon 90:10 our way.

But of course we had our detractors. When Liberal Senator George Brandis compared Kerry, me and the Greens in general to Nazis, John Howard supported him. To back his ludicrous claim, Brandis cited the works of two American academics, who promptly nailed him for misrepresenting their views. Neither Howard nor Brandis nor any of the senior Liberals he consulted before levelling his false attack – in the name of free speech – have apologised.

There was a recurrent theme in the response from the right. TV's crocodile handler Steve Irwin, who was invited to the Lodge for a barbecue after Bush's speech, was furious at my interjections: 'Oh crikey, mate, he needs to be taken out the back and given a good belting.' Others too were feeling physical. Sydney commercial radio's Alan

Jones: 'You feel like grabbing him and cracking him across the skull.' And Adelaide radio's Andrew Reimer: 'I'd like to grab Bob Brown for example and just ever so delicately lift my knee into his face about five times. Smash his nose and face in. That's what I'd like to do.'

Many of the hostile callers to radio, for whom rudeness was the main concern, felt ashamed. Along with US Ambassador Tom Schieffer, they had been excited 'like a little kid' at the President's visit and were embarrassed that such greatness could not be left beyond reproach. 'Bob Brown is a rude and arrogant man,' they claimed. 'The stunt by noxious weeds Bob Brown and Kerry Nettle was incorrect.' I was a 'goose' and a 'fool'. One Queenslander wrote to me:

> I have always known that you are a complete and utter ratbag, but your performance in parliament yesterday during the speech by George Bush was the limit. You are such a rude, uncouth person and the majority of the Australian population agree with me. As far as the two people being held in Guantanamao Bay are concerned, you are wrong in stating they are two Australians. One is an an Australian and the other is a Muslim. You say you are a proud Australian. Rubbish! I am a proud Australian and . . . you make me sick!

Very few people were undecided about our stand, but Sydney's *Manly Daily*, which circulates in Tony Abbott's seat of Warringah, had a well-balanced editorial to go with its front-page article on the role of Abbott – who called us 'publicity hounds' – in having Kerry and me banned from the House for Hu's speech:

> This was a rare opportunity for Greens senators Bob Brown and Kerry Nettle to take their party's consistent anti-war message beyond our borders. It was an equally rare chance for Mr Abbot to reinforce his Government's firm alliance with US foreign policy and President Bush . . . In truth, yesterday's gathering of "publicity hounds" (politicians) showed the world that Australia has a healthy, functioning and vibrant democracy of divergent views.

Most letters the Greens received took this point further. 'Thank you for being the only Australian political leader with the fortitude to stand up to George Bush,' wrote another Queenslander. 'I understand the redneck government of Australia's giving you a hard time at the moment but . . . the talk where I work today has been pro the Greens. I hope you never give up.'

'Congratulations and thank you, Senator. Thank you for your attempt to prove that at least some of our politicians are still human beings and have a backbone!' wrote one Victorian. Many other letters were in the same vein. 'Thank you and Senator Nettle for having the guts to stand up and be counted on behalf of decent Australians.' 'You did what a lot of people wanted to do. I admire you.' 'One small, passionate voice for humanity.' 'Let's get back to being true blue Australians.' 'Good on you, Bob Brown. I could not have sat through that twaddle without voicing my opinion.' 'Congratulations for what you've done. We need people with guts and you've got plenty. You won my vote!'

As a result of the CNN footage going around the world, we also received very supportive international mail, typified by this letter from Ontario, Canada:

> By demanding answers to the burning questions about the morality and legality of United States foreign policy, the world may demonstrate to the people of the USA that their government and military establishment has hijacked the principles of their constitution, and corroded and corrupted the moral fabric of the US to such an extent as to jeopardize the very existence of that once truly great country. Rare and precious indeed are those people who will stand in their place in a venerated house such as the Parliament of Australia and say in a straightforward way what is on their mind and what the world desperately needs to hear. Thank

you, Sir, you do a great service to the world, your country, and your constituents.

There are no absolutes in politics, but I was struck by the difference in style, not just in content, of the responses from our supporters and critics. From the former came more delayed, reasoned and peaceful comments; from the latter came outraged, kneejerk and inherently violent reactions. This disparity corresponds to the long-sighted and more humane policy base of the Greens, as against the short-sighted, self-oriented standpoint of conventional politics. Our interjections were driven by a desire to preserve the Australian parliament as the centre of our society's discourse, and to prevent it from being used as an exclusive pedestal for the established order, foreign powers and the rich. To the Greens, the defence of the human rights of powerless people, however far away in the world, is of greater importance than being obsequiously polite to those who are powerful and close up.

Herein lies a crucial dilemma for politics and global society in this age of weapons of mass destruction. The law of the ladder of political and business ascendancy is that those least worried about treading on other climbers will most readily get to the top. Yet what the world needs atop that ladder is humaneness and far-sightedness and understanding. The Greens will have to outdo the finger-trampling market fundamentalists who fear the world's complex fabric, a complexity that not even nuclear weaponry can simplify.

Howard's invitation to the capitalist Bush and the communist Hu to use our parliament as a stage was part of a new phenomenon in global politics whereby leaders assist each other in silencing the voices of dissent within their communities in order to promulgate the advance of the market. Dollars over democracy, in other words. Manners over human rights. The laws of etiquette over international laws.

Prior to his visit to Canberra, George Bush went to Manila, where five opposition members walked out on his speech. They broke the trail for Kerry and me, and our interjections further loosened the straightjacket of acquiescence to the presidential cavalcade. The global reaction showed that it's okay to speak up to the world's most powerful man.

By the time Bush got to London in November 2003, plans for him to address the houses of Westminster had been abandoned: the fear was too great that a flood of interjections from MPs who had opposed the war in Iraq would scupper the whole facade of presidential majesty so necessary for giving his deeply flawed brand of politics its veneer of legitimacy.

Natural Philanthropy: The Australian Bush Heritage Fund

In the winter of 1990 I became very anxious at the prospect of going into serious hock in order to buy two blocks of forest which were for sale near my home in the Liffey Valley. An area of 241 hectares – the equivalent of the same number of football fields – was at stake, and it was an investment that was to have dividends way beyond Liffey.

The Liffey Valley lies southwest of Launceston. When I arrived there in 1973 it was the cloud-wrapped turrets of Drys Bluff, rising 1000 metres above the valley, which struck me most. The bluff is such a hard climb that most locals had never done it. Only a few bushwalkers ever made the attempt. Some years later, I met Launceston forester Paul Smith who, besides inviting me on that fateful first rafting trip down the Franklin River in 1976, talked a lot about the definition of wilderness. To him, remoteness was a key factor. True wilderness is free of the impact of modern technology, and it is not until you are half a day's walk from a road that this is the case. Those areas around wilderness that provide the half-day's walk he called remoting zones – they may not be totally intact or out of technology's reach.

Drys Bluff is wilderness once you are over the top. There is a large tract of roadless, fenceless, buildingless plateau country on top that runs southwest to the Great Lake and west to the Lake Highway. The Central Plateau slopes south from the Great Western Tiers, of which Drys Bluff – at 1340 metres a little higher than Hobart's Mt Wellington – is the northeastern corner.

The remoteness of this wilderness is provided by the wild country between the Liffey Valley and those great dolerite turrets above. In days gone by, the steep bluff-side forests were the haunt of possum trappers and, on the lower slopes, sawmillers. Much of the forest was put to the match, and much more on the valley floor was ringbarked a century ago and left desolate, a scene of grey tree skeletons.

In 1978 I heard that the loggers were coming again. Unlike their predecessors who worked with horses, axes and primitive machinery (including a water-driven mill up the valley), the modern loggers had bulldozers, chainsaws and cables with which to cart logs up and down the most precipitous terrain. Concerned for the fate of the bluff, I worked with friends (Paul Smith was especially helpful) at the Tasmanian Conservation Trust in Launceston to put together a plan for a forest reserve. I kept my involvement off the record because I was by now campaigning with the Wilderness Society to stop the Franklin Dam and was therefore offside with the minister for forests. Much of the plan was taken up by the Forestry Commission and it so happened that one of the first acts of the conservative Gray government after its election in 1982, at the height of the Franklin-dam furore, was to declare the Drys Bluff Forest Reserve, along with the Liffey Falls Forest Reserve a little further to the west.

In 1989, under the Labor–Green Accord, the Drys Bluff Forest Reserve became the northeastern corner of the expanded Tasmanian Wilderness World Heritage Area. The Liffey Falls Reserve was included and there were moves afoot by local residents and conservation groups to make the whole of the Great Western Tiers a national park. Because of their height and east–west expanse, the Tiers have a great diversity of climate, vegetation, animal life and geological history. There are fossils in my back paddock.

Then, in mid-1990, the two large, privately owned blocks on the flank of Drys Bluff, adjacent to but outside the reserves, came up for sale. The logging companies were after them and there was a risk that the forests would be clearfelled. Besides supporting diverse eucalypt forests with a galaxy of wildlife, including a pair of red-eyed white goshawks, these blocks were a key to keeping the bluff's remoteness intact. They lay between the farms and the plateau wilderness, between the roaring bitumen and profound silence, between the late twentieth century and the ancient world of nature up on the plateau.

Just above the blocks, I came upon a rainforested gully with a carpet of ferns interspersed with sandstone boulders which had toppled down from the cliffs. A small creek bubbled between the ferns. In a wide dry space beneath one of the boulders I found some tiny, hand-worked shards of stone: the Aborigines had lived here, 750 metres up, facing the morning sun. They called the bluff Tayhtikitheeker – today we don't even know what that musical word, or sentence, means. I decided I had to take the risk and try to buy this land.

The blocks could fetch $250 000 or more, so I went to see my bank manager and arranged to mortgage my house. I would have to commit to a big fundraising effort over the next six months in order to repay the money. As parliament was sitting in Hobart on the day of the auction, which was in Launceston, a friend bid for me. I spent that day full of trepidation about the prospect of so much debt, but even more anxious that the bid would fail. At last the call came through: I got the two blocks at the reserve price of $250 000. I had both the forests and a whopping debt.

That evening a woodchipping company officer called

the real-estate agent to ask if the Dr Brown who had purchased the forests was 'that environmentalist Dr Brown'. In the company's reckoning, the forests were worth $400000 as woodchips. I could have cleaned up $150000 by capitalising on my new assets, but, alas, the company never called!

The purchase of the Liffey forests was made possible by my windfall of $49000 from the 1990 Goldman Environmental Prize. With this money as a deposit, there remained a further $201000 to be paid, and I got together with a group of Hobart friends to set up a fund to raise the money. Some put in their life savings as an interest-free loan. After head-scratching, we called the group the Australian Bush Heritage Fund. Graphic artist Ian Skinner donated an eye-catching logo.

From the outset, we aimed at raising money beyond the Liffey debt in order to buy and protect other land of environmental value around Australia. It became a proposal for private or community-owned national parks, for the enjoyment of people for all time. We didn't expect quick results: philanthropy in Australia is a relatively young social innovation, unlike in the United States where it has a much longer history. In 1951 in the US, the Nature Conservancy was set up to buy land throughout the Americas. It depends on philanthropy, and in 2001–02 alone had a budget close to US$1 billion.

In 1991–92 the Australian Bush Heritage Fund

received a total of $34 483 in donations. It took years to repay the Liffey debt, but in the meantime more people had loaned the balance of the money free of interest. Within three years we had a reassuring list of donors, along with a room nestled in the Tasmanian Conservation Trust's Hobart offices. By 1994 we had employed a part-time staffer and invested in an 8-hectare block of fan-palm rainforest, also the habitat of the endangered cassowary, adjoining Queensland's Daintree Wet Tropics World Heritage Area.

Thirteen years on, Bush Heritage has a highly skilled staff of fifteen, an annual turnover of $3 million, and a multi-talented board of unpaid directors. It has acquired eighteen properties around Australia. To the Liffey and Daintree purchases have been added:

- 120 hectares of rare dry rainforest in the Bega Valley, New South Wales
- the 400-hectare pristine Erith Island in Bass Strait, which has since been given to Tasmania as part of the Kent Group National Park
- 389 hectares of wandoo woodland and wildflower land at Kojonup, Western Australia
- 140 hectares of untouched coastal heathland fringing Saltwater Lagoon at Tasmania's Friendly Beaches, adjoining the national park created by the Labor–Green Accord

- 593 hectares of brigalow woodlands and koala habitat at Goonderoo, Queensland
- 7 hectares protecting the largest remaining stand of South Esk Pine at Apsley River, Tasmania, and honouring Ros Jones, an eighteen-year-old who accidentally drowned during the Franklin River campaign
- 432 hectares protecting the largest remaining grassy whitebox woodland at Tarcutta, New South Wales
- 411 hectares of donated escarpment forest, home to sugar- and squirrel-gliders, in the upper reaches of the Shoalhaven River, New South Wales
- 59 000 hectares at Carnarvon Station Reserve, linking two national parks in the headwaters of the Warrego River, Queensland
- 4 hectares of wildlife-rich donated rainforest – the Currumbin Valley Reserve – behind Queensland's Gold Coast
- 877 hectares of kwongan heath, a mallee-fowl habitat, at Chereninup, Western Australia
- 68 619 magnificent hectares of york and salmon gums at Charles Darwin Reserve, north of the wheat-belt town of Dalwallinu, Western Australia
- 20 hectares of sandstone and ferny-waterfall country high on Drys Bluff. This third block in the Liffey Valley was donated in 2003 by Judy Henderson, who helped set up Bush Heritage
- Ethabuka Station, the largest acquisition at 214 000

hectares, which adjoins the Simpson Desert National Park in southwest Queensland – a refuge for a dozen endangered species, including the white-bellied mulgara, a marsupial carnivore that feeds on the outback's insects

- and, in 2004, the lease on Hunter Island in Bass Strait: 6300 hectares of rare coastal heath and woodland, ancient Aboriginal cave habitat, and a mid-migration feeding ground for the critically endangered orange-bellied parrot.

These hundreds of thousands of hectares across Australia are rich in rare fauna and flora: frogs, orchids, ferns, beetles, kangaroos and platypuses. Each reserve is part of a rapidly disappearing Australia which is under threat from land-clearing, urban sprawl, global warming and introduced pests and diseases. The Bush Heritage properties are strongholds for the nation's wildlife, managed by a remarkably lively and dedicated staff who obviously enjoy their work.

How could such an enterprise go wrong? In the United States it happened easily. The Nature Conservancy, on which Bush Heritage was modelled, has grown to be the world's richest environment group, with US$3 billion in assets. It has received single gifts of more than US$100 million. The Nature Conservancy is affectionately called Big Green and has hundreds of dedicated employees.

However, in recent years the Conservancy has been racked by controversy, despite its great work, and there have been stories in the press about development on its lands, such as natural-gas extraction, a housing estate and logging. All these cases are extremely complicated: sometimes rescued lands are already suffering commercial exploitation. The troubles are not new; a decade ago one Nature Conservancy clod famously quipped that donated money 'may be tainted money but it ain't enough!'

It hasn't helped that the Nature Conservancy's board is made up of executives of large corporations, including oil corporations, which hardly have an environmental outlook. There's one particular story, concerning Attwater's prairie chicken, that's worth looking at. This very large chicken featured in the 2003 Academy Award-winning documentary, *Travelling Birds*. The male has a stunning courtship ritual marked by cocked tail feathers, inflated orange cheeks, and a great deal of strutting and vocal duelling with competitors. A century ago, there were a million Attwater's prairie chickens on Texas's Gulf Coast. By 1937 there were 8700, by 1967 there were 1100, and by 1992 just forty-six.

The Washington Post of 5 May 2001 ran a story headlined 'How a Bid to Save a Species Came to Grief'. It reported that in 1993 the Nature Conservancy received one of its largest corporate donations in the form of a piece of Texas prairie land that included the last remaining breeding grounds of the chicken. The donation was made by Mobil Oil. The Nature Conservancy then proceeded to drill for gas under the nesting grounds.

The article claimed that the Conservancy adheres to an aggressive form of 'compatible development', whereby it seeks to meet both business and ecological needs. And whereas the Conservancy had intended the reserve to prove that drilling can be carried out without harming the environment, and also intended to use the profits to purchase additional habitat for the birds, by 2001 there were fewer Attwater's prairie chickens on the land than there had been before the drilling began.

The argument about the impact on the prairie chickens of the gas drilling, and the resulting pipeline that was required to carry gas to an interstate line, is complex, and the Nature Conservancy has criticised *The Washington Post* for 'focussing on a narrow set of isolated problems' that do not 'present an honest or comprehensive picture of the work of the Conservancy'. But the lesson here is an important one, and, unlike the Nature Conservancy, the Australian Bush Heritage Fund has no directors of big corporations on its board, and hopefully it never will. What it has, in abundance, is a rapidly growing band of donors and volunteers, who, like me, get great joy out of the way in which it is permanently protecting some of Australia's most wild and beautiful places.

You can call the Australian Bush Heritage Fund

on freecall 1800 677 101, or visit its website at www.bushheritage.org: any advice will be gratefully received, and donations are tax-deductible.

My home and its 11 hectares beside the Liffey River are assigned to Bush Heritage in my will. This ensures the protection of a little more forest and white-goshawk territory under those lofty turrets of Drys Bluff, where one day long ago, while out walking, I decided to go into hock for the land and its wildlife.

A 10-POINT PLAN FOR FUTURE PRIME MINISTERS

How to make Australia a proud, compassionate, independent nation

1   Commit to guaranteed, free, quality public education from pre-school to university, which means ending the HECS scheme

2   Guarantee a universal public health scheme, ensuring access for all to a family doctor, dentist, mental health professional and hospital

3   Make Australia a world environmental leader by protecting old-growth forests, woodlands and grasslands, restoring our rivers, ratifying the Kyoto Protocol, and investing in clean, efficient public transport

4   Give Australia back its humanity, and save taxpayers hundreds of millions of dollars annually, by closing down the long-stay detention centres and ending temporary protection visas

5   Abandon the US–Australia free-trade agreement, which will leave Australia disadvantaged by threatening our environmental and quarantine safeguards and our public utilities while not removing US agricultural protections

6   End Australia's involvement in the war in Iraq by bringing home our troops
7   Return to the belief in multiculturalism and develop an independent foreign policy, rather than continue subservience to the White House
8   Give justice to Australia's first peoples: rekindle the plan for national land-rights legislation abandoned by Bob Hawke
9   Drop plans to disempower the Senate and instead campaign energetically for a democratic Australian republic
10 Lead a global effort to divert some of the US$1 trillion annual weapons budget, so that every child on Earth has food, clean water and a school to attend.

With thanks to Ben Oquist

CHARTER OF THE GLOBAL GREENS

Adopted by the Global Greens Conference in Canberra, 2001.
The Global Greens is the international network of Green
parties and political movements. This charter can be found at
www.global.greens.org.au

PREAMBLE

We, as citizens of the planet and members of the Global Greens,

United in our awareness that we depend on the Earth's vitality,
diversity and beauty, and that it is our responsibility to pass them on,
undiminished or even improved, to the next generation,
Recognising that the dominant patterns of human production and
consumption, based on the dogma of economic growth at any cost
and the excessive and wasteful use of natural resources without
considering the Earth's carrying capacity, are causing extreme
deterioration in the environment and a massive extinction of species,
Acknowledging that injustice, racism, poverty, ignorance, corruption,
crime and violence, armed conflict and the search for maximum
short-term profit are causing widespread human suffering,
Accepting that developed countries through their pursuit of
economic and political goals have contributed to the degradation of
the environment and of human dignity,
Understanding that many of the world's peoples and nations
have been impoverished by the long centuries of colonisation and
exploitation, creating an ecological debt owed by the rich nations to
those that have been impoverished,
Committed to closing the gap between rich and poor and building a
citizenship based on equal rights for all individuals in all spheres of
social, economic, political and cultural life,
Recognising that without equality between men and women, no real
democracy can be achieved,

Concerned for the dignity of humanity and the value of cultural heritage,
Recognising the rights of indigenous people and their contribution
to the common heritage, as well as the right of all minorities and
oppressed peoples to their culture, religion, economic and cultural
life,
Convinced that cooperation rather than competition is a pre-
requisite for ensuring the guarantee of such human rights as
nutritious food, comfortable shelter, health, education, fair labour,
free speech, clean air, potable water and an unspoilt natural
environment,
Recognising that the environment ignores borders between countries and
Building on the Declaration of the Global Gathering of Greens at
Rio in 1992,

Assert the need for fundamental changes in people's attitudes, values,
and ways of producing and living,
Declare that the new millennium provides a defining point to begin
that transformation,
Resolve to promote a comprehensive concept of sustainability which:
- protects and restores the integrity of the Earth's ecosystems, with
  special concern for biodiversity and the natural processes that
  sustain life
- acknowledges the interrelatedness of all ecological, social and
  economic processes
- balances individual interests with the common good
- harmonises freedom with responsibility
- welcomes diversity within unity
- reconciles short-term objectives with long-term goals
- ensures that future generations have the same right as the present
  generation to natural and cultural benefits,
Affirm our responsibility to one another, to the greater community
of life, and to future generations,
Commit ourselves as Green parties and political movements from
around the world to implement these interrelated principles and to
create a global partnership in support of their fulfilment.

PRINCIPLES

The policies of the Global Greens are founded upon the principles of:

Ecological Wisdom

We acknowledge that human beings are part of the natural world and we respect the specific values of all forms of life, including non-human species.

We acknowledge the wisdom of the indigenous peoples of the world, as custodians of the land and its resources.

We acknowledge that human society depends on the ecological resources of the planet, and must ensure the integrity of ecosystems and preserve biodiversity and the resilience of life-supporting systems.

This requires:

- that we learn to live within the ecological and resource limits of the planet
- that we protect animal and plant life, and life itself that is sustained by the natural elements: earth, water, air and sun
- where knowledge is limited, that we take the path of caution, in order to secure the continued abundance of the resources of the planet for present and future generations.

Social Justice

We assert that the key to social justice is the equitable distribution of social and natural resources, both locally and globally, to meet basic human needs unconditionally, and to ensure that all citizens have full opportunities for personal and social development.

We declare that there is no social justice without environmental justice, and no environmental justice without social justice.

This requires:

- a just organisation of the world and a stable world economy which will close the widening gap between rich and poor, both within and between countries; balance the flow of resources from South to North; and lift the burden of debt on poor countries which prevents their development.
- the eradication of poverty, as an ethical, social, economic, and ecological imperative
- the elimination of illiteracy

- a new vision of citizenship built on equal rights for all individuals regardless of gender, race, age, religion, class, ethnic or national origin, sexual orientation, disability, wealth or health.

Participatory Democracy

We strive for a democracy in which all citizens have the right to express their views, and are able to directly participate in the environmental, economic, social and political decisions which affect their lives; so that power and responsibility are concentrated in local and regional communities, and devolved only where essential to higher tiers of governance.

This requires:

- individual empowerment through access to all the relevant information required for any decision, and access to education to enable all to participate
- breaking down inequalities of wealth and power that inhibit participation
- building grassroots institutions that enable decisions to be made directly at the appropriate level by those affected, based on systems which encourage civic vitality, voluntary action and community responsibility
- strong support for giving young people a voice through educating, encouraging and assisting youth involvement in every aspect of political life, including their participation in all decision-making bodies
- that all elected representatives are committed to the principles of transparency, truthfulness, and accountability in governance
- that all electoral systems are transparent and democratic, and that this is enforced by law
- that in all electoral systems, each adult has an equal vote
- that all electoral systems are based on proportional representation, and all elections are publicly funded with strict limits on, and full transparency of, corporate and private donations
- that all citizens have the right to be a member of the political party of their choice within a multi-party system.

Nonviolence

We declare our commitment to nonviolence and strive for a culture of peace and cooperation between states, inside societies and between individuals, as the basis of global security.

We believe that security should not rest mainly on military strength but on cooperation, sound economic and social development, environmental safety, and respect for human rights. This requires:

- a comprehensive concept of global security, which gives priority to social, economic, ecological, psychological and cultural aspects of conflict, instead of a concept based primarily on military balances of power
- a global security system capable of the prevention, management and resolution of conflicts
- removing the causes of war by understanding and respecting other cultures, eradicating racism, promoting freedom and democracy, and ending global poverty
- pursuing general and complete disarmament, including international agreements to ensure a complete and definitive ban of nuclear, biological and chemical arms, anti-personnel mines and depleted uranium weapons
- strengthening the United Nations (UN) as the global organisation of conflict management and peacekeeping
- pursuing a rigorous code of conduct on arms exports to countries where human rights are being violated.

Sustainability

We recognise the limited scope for the material expansion of human society within the biosphere, and the need to maintain biodiversity through sustainable use of renewable resources and responsible use of non-renewable resources.

We believe that to achieve sustainability, and in order to provide for the needs of present and future generations within the finite resources of the Earth, continuing growth in global consumption, population and material inequity must be halted and reversed.

We recognise that sustainability will not be possible as long as poverty persists.

This requires:

- ensuring that the rich limit their consumption to allow the poor their fair share of the Earth's resources
- redefining the concept of wealth, to focus on quality of life rather than capacity for over-consumption
- creating a world economy which aims to satisfy the needs of

all, not the greed of a few; and enables those presently living to meet their own needs, without jeopardising the ability of future generations to meet theirs

- eliminating the causes of population growth by ensuring economic security, and providing access to basic education and health, for all; giving both men and women greater control over their fertility
- redefining the roles and responsibilities of trans-national corporations in order to support the principles of sustainable development
- implementing mechanisms to tax, as well as regulating, speculative financial flows
- ensuring that market prices of goods and services fully incorporate the environmental costs of their production and consumption
- achieving greater resource and energy efficiency and development and use of environmentally sustainable technologies
- encouraging local self-reliance to the greatest practical extent to create worthwhile, satisfying communities
- recognising the key role of youth culture and encouraging an ethic of sustainability within that culture.

Respect for Diversity

We honour cultural, linguistic, ethnic, sexual, religious and spiritual diversity within the context of individual responsibility toward all beings.

We defend the right of all persons, without discrimination, to an environment supportive of their dignity, bodily health, and spiritual well-being.

We promote the building of respectful, positive and responsible relationships across lines of division in the spirit of a multi-cultural society.

This requires:

- recognition of the rights of indigenous peoples to the basic means of their survival, both economic and cultural, including rights to land and to self-determination; and acknowledgment of their contribution to the common heritage of national and global culture
- recognition of the rights of ethnic minorities to develop their culture, religion and language without discrimination, and to full legal, social and cultural participation in the democratic process

- recognition of and respect for sexual minorities
- equality between women and men in all spheres of social, economic, political and cultural life
- significant involvement of youth culture as a valuable contribution to our Green vision, and recognition that young people have distinct needs and modes of expression.

POLITICAL ACTION

1. Democracy
1.0 The majority of the world's people live in countries with undemocratic regimes where corruption is rampant and human-rights abuses and press censorship are commonplace. Developed democracies suffer less apparent forms of corruption through media concentration, corporate political funding, systematic exclusion of racial, ethnic, national and religious communities, and electoral systems that discriminate against alternative ideas and new and small parties.

The Greens –
1.1 Have as a priority the encouragement and support of grassroots movements and other organisations of civil society working for democratic, transparent and accountable government, at all levels from local to global.
1.2 Actively support giving young people a voice through educating, encouraging and assisting youth participation in every aspect of political action.
1.3 Will strive for the democratisation of gender relations by promoting appropriate mediations to enable women and men equally to take part in the economic, political and social spheres.
1.4 Urge immediate ratification of the Organisation for Economic Cooperation and Development (OECD) Convention on Combating Bribery of Foreign Public Officials in International Business.
1.5 Uphold the right of citizens to have access to official information and to free and independent media.
1.6 Will work for universal access to electronic communications and information technology: as a minimum, radio, and community-

based internet and email. We will also work to make access to these technologies as cheap as possible.

1.7 Uphold a just, secular legal system that ensures the right of defence and practises proportionality between crime and punishment.

1.8 Support the public funding of elections, and ensure all donations, where permitted, are fully transparent, with a limit on donations from both individuals and corporations.

1.9 Will challenge corporate domination of government, especially where citizens are deprived of their right to political participation.

1.10 Support the separation of powers between the executive, legislative and judicial systems, and the separation of state and religion.

1.11 Support the development and strengthening of local government.

1.12 Support the restructuring of state institutions to democratise them and make them more transparent and efficient in serving the goal of citizens' power and sustainable development.

2. Equity

2.0 The differences in living standards and opportunities in the world today are intolerable. Third World debt is at an all-time high of $2.5 trillion, while Organisation of Economic Cooperation and Development (OECD) countries give just 0.23% of GNP in aid. The richest 20% of the world's population has over 80% of the income while 1.2 billion people live in poverty (on less than a dollar a day). 125 million children never attend school and 880 million people can neither read nor write – more than two-thirds of these are women, as are 60% of the poor. Population growth has slowed but is still expected to add another 2–3 billion people by 2050. Human Immunodeficiency Virus (HIV) and tuberculosis (TB) infections are increasing.

The Greens –

2.1 Will work to increase government aid to developing countries, and support aid funding being directed to the poorest of the poor, with the priorities being determined through working with local communities.

2.2 Will work to improve the rights, status, education and political participation of women.

2.3 Commit ourselves to the goal of making high-quality primary education universal by 2015, financed through increased aid and debt relief.

2.4 Will work towards cancellation of developing-country debt, especially in the poorest countries, and support the use of incentives to ensure that savings from debt relief are channelled into poverty reduction and environment conservation, and that transparent and accountable processes are in place, with participation from affected communities.

2.5 See concerted action to combat the great pandemics, including HIV-Aids, TB and malaria, as a priority, especially in Africa, where a twofold effort is needed to allow general access to low-cost and efficient therapies, and to restore economic progress, especially through education.

2.6 Recognise the right to compensation of those people that lose access to their natural resources through displacement by environmental destruction or human intervention, such as colonisation and migration.

2.7 Will review the relationship between exclusive ownership of property and exclusive use of its resources, with a view to curbing environmental abuse and extending access for basic livelihood to all, especially indigenous communities.

2.8 Will work to ensure that all men, women and children can achieve economic security without recourse to personally damaging activities, such as pornography, prostitution or the sale of organs.

2.9 Will commit to work for more equal allocation of welfare and for creation of equal opportunities inside all our societies, recognising that there is a growing number of poor and marginalised people in developed countries also.

2.10 Will defend and promote the human, social and environmental rights of people of colour.

3. Climate Change and Energy

3.0 Nine of the ten warmest years on record were in the 1990s. The level of CO_2 in the atmosphere is higher than at any time in the last 15 million years. The frequency of climatic disasters is increasing, killing thousands and displacing millions of people. Widespread bleaching and death of coral reefs, which first occurred in 1998, will become commonplace within 20 years. Scientists from the Intergovernmental Panel on Climate Change (IPCC) state that global warming is real, and that human action is a substantial factor in the change. The Earth is expected to warm by a further 1–5°C this century, and sea-level rise, which has already started, will continue for the next 500 years, flooding many of the Earth's most populated regions. Climate catastrophe looms unless we act now.

The Greens –

3.1 Adopt the target of limiting CO_2 levels in the atmosphere to 450 ppm in the shortest period possible, as requested by the IPCC. Developed countries will have to fulfil not only the Kyoto Protocol (-5.2% of 1990 levels by 2010 globally, -8% for the EU, -6% for the USA), which even if it is a step in the right direction is grossly insufficient, but also achieve a reduction between -20% to -30% by 2020 in order that a target of -70% to -90% may be reached by the end of the century. In addition, action must be taken to reduce the emissions of the other greenhouse gases.

3.2 Urge the coming into force of the Kyoto Protocol in line with this target, and insist that the implementation rules lead to real emission reductions from industrial sources by developed countries, including a system of penalties for non-compliance.

3.3 Will work to establish an international emissions reporting framework for transnational corporations, linked to global carbon taxes and global environmental loads.

3.4 Will work hard to ensure that developing countries have access to the most efficient, sustainable and appropriate technology, with a strong focus on renewable energy, and that they agree to Climate Change Conventions to ensure that actions are comprehensive and worldwide. The equity principle must be at the core of climate-change negotiations and measures.

3.5 Oppose any expansion of nuclear power and will work to phase it out rapidly.

3.6 Will support a call for a moratorium on new fossil fuel exploration and development.

3.7 Oppose clearing and logging of old-growth forests, noting that they are the most carbon rich ecosystems on the planet, vital to indigenous people, rich in plants and animals, and irreplaceable in any human time scale.

3.8 Promote tree planting of diverse species but not monocultures, as a short-term measure for carbon sequestration, with other benefits for the environment.

3.9 Promote the levying of taxes on non-renewable energy and the use of funds raised to promote energy efficiency and renewable energy.

3.10 Support research into the use of sustainable energy sources and the technical development of ecological power production.

3.11 Promote energy-efficient technologies and green-power infrastructure between and within countries and economies on a no-costs or minimal-costs basis. This is one of the economic costs of the emissions to date by western countries.

4. Biodiversity

4.0 Healthy ecosystems are essential to human life, yet we seem to have forgotten the relationship between nature and society. Extinction rates are 100 to 1000 times higher than in pre-human times. Only 20% of the Earth's original forests remain relatively undisturbed. Sixty per cent of fish stocks are in danger of being overfished. Invasions by non-native plants, animals and diseases are growing rapidly. Habitat destruction and species extinction are driven by industrial and agricultural development that also exacerbates climate change, global inequity and the destruction of indigenous cultures and livelihoods. Agricultural monoculture, promoted by agribusiness and accelerated by genetic modification and patenting of nature, threatens the diversity of crop and domestic animal species, radically increasing vulnerability to disease.

The Greens –
4.1 Will vigorously oppose environmentally destructive agricultural and industrial development and give primary effort to protecting native plants and animals in their natural habitat, and wherever possible in large tracts.
4.2 Will work to remove subsidies for environmentally destructive activities, including logging, fossil fuel exploitation, dam construction, mining, genetic engineering and agricultural monoculture.
4.3 Will promote ecological purchasing policies, for products such as wood, based only on the most rigorous definition of sustainability backed by credible labelling.
4.4 Support the concept of 'debt for nature' swaps, subject to the agreement of affected indigenous and local communities.
4.5 Will promote the repair of degraded natural environments, and the clean-up of toxic sites of former and existing military and industrial zones around the world.
4.6 Note that reducing the transport of goods around the world, in line with a preference for local production where possible, will have the added benefit of reducing 'bio-invasions', as well as reducing fossil fuel consumption and greenhouse gas emissions.

4.7 Commit to promote a global ecology curriculum for all levels of education.

4.8 Will work towards establishing an international court of justice specific for environmental destruction and the loss of biodiversity where cases can be heard against corporations, national states and individuals.

4.9 Will refuse to accept the patenting and merchandising of life.

5. Governing economic globalisation by sustainability principles

5.0 Fifty of the 100 biggest economies in the world today are corporations. With the collusion of governments, they have created a legal system that puts unfettered economic activity above the public good, protects corporate welfare but attacks social welfare, and makes national economies subservient to a global financial casino that turns over $US1.3 trillion per day in speculative transactions. However, the tide may be turning. The Multilateral Agreement on Investment was defeated for the time being. In developed countries international financial institutions can meet only under siege conditions. The reputation of the World Bank and the International Monetary Fund (IMF) is in tatters.

The Greens –

5.1 Affirm that essentials of life, such as water, must remain publicly owned and controlled; and that culture, basic access to food, social and public health, education, and a free media are not 'commodities' to be subjected to international market agreements.

5.2 Support the creation of a World Environment Organisation by combining the United Nations Environment Program (UNEP), the United Nations Development Program (UNDP), and the Global Environment Facility (GEF) into a single institution with funding and power to impose sanctions to promote global sustainable development. The World Trade Organisation (WTO) should be subject to the decisions of this body.

5.3 Support abolition of the World Bank and IMF unless they are reformed so that their membership and decision-making are democratic, and their operations subservient to sustainability principles and to all international conventions on human and labour rights, and environmental protection.

5.4 Support abolition of the WTO unless it is reformed to make sustainability its central goal, supported by transparent and democratic processes and the participation of representatives from affected communities. In addition there must be separation of powers to remove the disputes settlement mechanism from the exclusive competence of the WTO. A sustainability impact assessment of earlier Negotiation Rounds is required before any new steps are taken.

5.5 Will work to prevent the implementation of new regional or hemispheric trade and investment agreements under the WTO rules – such as the proposed Free Trade Agreement of the Americas – but support countries' integration processes that assure people's welfare and environmental sustainability.

5.6 Will create a world environment where financial and economic institutions and organisations will nurture and protect environmentally sustainable projects that will sustain communities at all levels (local, regional, national and international).

5.7 Demand that international agreements on the environment, labour conditions and health should take precedence over any international rules on trade.

5.8 Will work to implement a Tobin-Henderson tax and other instruments to curb speculative international currency transactions and help encourage investment in the real economy, and to create funds to promote equity in global development.

5.9 Will work to require corporations to abide by the environmental, labour and social laws of their own country and of the country in which they are operating, whichever are the more stringent.

5.10 Will work to ensure that all global organisations, especially those with significant capacity to define the rules of international trade, firmly adhere to principles of sustainable development and pursue a training program of cultural change to fully realise this goal.

5.11 Want corporate welfare made transparent and subject to the same level of accountability as social welfare, with subsidies to environmentally and socially destructive activities phased out altogether.

5.12 Endorse the development of civic entrepreneurship to promote a community-based economy as a way of combating social exclusion caused by economic globalisation.

6. Human rights

6.0 Denial of human rights and freedoms goes hand in hand with poverty and political powerlessness. Millions suffer discrimination, intimidation, arbitrary detention, violence and death. Three-quarters of the world's governments have used torture in the last three years.

The Greens –

6.1 Endorse the Universal Declaration of Human Rights, the International Covenant on Economic, Social and Cultural Rights, the International Covenant on Civil and Political Rights, International Labour Organisation (ILO) conventions, and other international instruments for the protection of rights and freedoms. We believe that these rights are universal and indivisible and that national governments are responsible for upholding them.

6.2 Condemn all dictatorships and regimes which deny human rights, regardless of their political claims.

6.3 Will work with local communities to promote awareness of human rights, and to ensure that the UN Commission for Human Rights and other treaty bodies are adequately resourced.

6.4 Call for the Universal Declaration of Human Rights to be amended to include rights to a healthy natural environment and intergenerational rights to natural and cultural resources.

6.5 Uphold the right of women to make their own decisions, including the control of their fertility by the means they deem appropriate, free from discrimination or coercion, and will work to have the Convention on the Elimination of Discrimination Against Women (CEDAW) ratified, to remove reservations, and to bring the Optional Protocol into force.

6.6 Support the right of indigenous peoples to self-determination, land rights, and access to traditional hunting and fishing rights for their own subsistence, using humane and ecologically sustainable techniques; and support moves for indigenous people to set up and work through their own international bodies.

6.7 Call for the immediate adoption of the 1993 Draft Declaration on the Rights of Indigenous Peoples as the minimum standard of protection accepted by indigenous peoples, and support moves for indigenous people to set up and work through their own international bodies.

6.8 Demand that torturers are held accountable, and will campaign

for them to be brought to justice, in their own countries or
elsewhere, before an international panel of judges serving under the
auspices of the International Court of Justice.

6.9 Oppose any violation of the physical integrity of the individual
by torture, punishment or any other practices, including traditional
and religious mutilation.

6.10 Demand that the death penalty be abolished worldwide.

6.11 Call for governments to ensure that all asylum-seekers, whether
they are victims of state violence or independent armed groups, are
correctly treated in accordance with the 1951 Geneva Convention
on the Rights to Asylum; have access to fair processes; are not
arbitrarily detained; and are not returned to a country where they
might suffer violations of their fundamental human rights, or face
the risk of death, torture, or other inhuman treatment.

6.12 Call for the prohibition of collective expulsion.

6.13 Uphold the right of all workers to safe, fairly remunerated
employment, with the freedom to unionise.

6.14 Support the right of children to grow up free from the need
to work, and the establishment of a lower age limit for working
children/adolescents.

6.15 Demand decriminalisation of homosexuality, and support the
right of gay and lesbian people to their lifestyle, and the equal rights
of homosexual relationships.

6.16 Will work to improve the opportunities of disabled people
to live and work equally in society, including true political
participation.

6.17 Support the right of linguistic minorities to use their own
language.

7. Food and water

7.0 Hundreds of millions of people remain undernourished, not
because there is insufficient food but because of unequal access to
land, water, credit and markets. Genetically modified organisms
(GMOs) are not the solution, because the immediate problem is not
production but distribution. Moreover, GMOs pose unacceptable
risks to the environment, independent smaller farmers, and
consumers, as well as to the biodiversity that is our best insurance
against agricultural disaster. Water shortages loom, both in above-
ground systems and subterranean aquifers. Deforestation of

catchments takes a devastating toll in landslides and floods, while desertification and degradation are rapidly expanding. One bright spot is the rapid growth of organic agriculture.

The Greens –

7.1 Consider that access to clean water for basic needs is a fundamental right, and oppose the privatisation of water resources and infrastructure.

7.2 Will work to eliminate water subsidies, other than social subsidies, and to make water use more efficient.

7.3 Will work to ensure that fresh water and underground water resources are conserved in quality and quantity and are appropriately priced to ensure these resources are adequately protected from depletion.

7.4 Consider that the stability of catchments and the health of river systems is paramount, and will work with the people directly affected to stop the degradation of rivers, including new large dams and irrigation projects, and deforestation of catchments.

7.5 Will work with local communities in arid and semi-arid regions, where climate is dominated by uncertainty, to reduce land degradation.

7.6 Express their concern for countries that have been hard hit by desertification and deforestation, and ask the countries that have not yet done so to ratify the UN Convention of Desertification, and make the necessary resources available to enact this Convention.

7.7 Will support and promote organic agriculture.

7.8 Call for an international moratorium on the commercial growing of genetically modified crops for at least five years, pending research and debate, and establishment of regulatory systems, including company liability for adverse effects.

7.9 Will work to ensure that food is safe, with stringent regulations on production, storage and sale.

7.10 Will work to ensure that scientific research is conducted ethically and applied in accordance with the precautionary principle.

7.11 Call for a phase-out of all persistent and bio-accumulative manmade chemicals and to work to eliminate all releases to the environment of hazardous chemicals.

7.12 Will work to ensure that animal-growth hormones are banned, and stringent regulations governing the use of antibiotics on animals are enforced.

8. Sustainable planning

8.0 Consumption in industrialised countries is excessive by any measure, and largely responsible for environmental decline. People in western countries use 9 times as much paper as people in the South, and have 100 times as many cars per capita as people in China and India, for example. Changing to a green economy – which mimics ecological processes, eliminates waste by reusing and recycling materials, and emphasises activities that enhance the quality of life and relationships rather than the consumption of goods – promises new jobs, industries with less pollution, better work environments and a higher quality of life.

The Greens –

8.1 Promote measures of wellbeing rather than GDP to measure progress.

8.2 Consider that citizens of countries affected by a development project have the right to participate in decisions about it, regardless of national boundaries.

8.3 Will work to ensure that those who profit from exploiting any common and/or natural resources should pay the full market rent for the use of these resources, and for any damage they do to any other common resources.

8.4 Recognise that the impact of continuing urban growth (sprawl) onto agricultural land and the natural environment must be limited and ultimately stopped.

8.5 Recognise that the process of urbanisation due to rural poverty must be slowed and reversed through appropriate rural development programs which recognise the concept of limits to growth and protect the character and ecology of the rural landscape.

8.6 Support local planning for ecologically sustainable business, housing, transport, waste management, parks, city forests and public spaces; and will establish links between Greens at local and regional level around the planet to exchange information and support.

8.7 Will work to reduce vehicle-based urban pollution by opposing ever-expanding freeways; encouraging the use of energy-efficient vehicles; integrating land-use planning with public transport, bicycling and walking; prioritising mass-transit planning and funding over private-auto infrastructure; and eliminating tax policies that favour auto-centric development.

8.8 Will work to create socially responsible economic strategies, using taxes and public finance to maximise incentives for fair distribution of wealth, and eco-taxes to provide incentives to avoid waste and pollution.

8.9 Demand that corporations and communities reduce, reuse and recycle waste, aiming for a zero-waste economy which replicates a natural ecosystem.

8.10 Will support all policies that allow countries to increase job creation through economic activities that add value, or through recycling of resources, the production of durable goods, organic agriculture, renewable energy and environmental protection.

8.11 Promote socially responsible investment and ecological marketing so that consumers can make positive choices based on reliable information.

8.12 Recognise the value of traditional and local knowledge and beliefs, and support its incorporation into planning and projects.

9. Peace and security

9.0 The causes of conflict are changing. The distinctions between war, organised crime and deliberate large-scale abuses of human rights are becoming increasingly blurred; and the arms trade is growing and globalising, nourished by a unique exemption from WTO rules against subsidies. As a global network, we have a vital role to play in strengthening the links between community organisations working for human rights and peace, and supporting and shaping the emerging concepts and institutions of global governance.

The Greens –

9.1 Support strengthening the role of the UN as a global organisation of conflict management and peacekeeping, while, noting that, where prevention fails and in situations of structural and massive violations of human rights and/or genocide, the use of force may be justified if it is the only means of preventing further human-rights violations and suffering, provided that it is used under a mandate from the UN. Nonetheless, individual countries have the right not to support or to cooperate with the action.

9.2 Will campaign for greater power for countries of the South in the UN, by working to abolish the veto power in the Security Council, to remove the category of permanent membership of it, and to increase the number of states with membership.

9.3 Support the proposed International Criminal Court. Mass rape should be regarded as a war crime.

9.4 Seek to curtail the power of the military-industrial-financial complex in order to radically reduce the trade in armaments, ensure transparency of manufacturing and remove hidden subsidies that benefit the military industries.

9.5 Will work to regulate and reduce, with the long-term aim of eliminating, the international arms trade (including banning nuclear, biological and chemical arms, depleted-uranium weapons and anti-personnel mines) and bring it within the ambit of the UN.

9.6 Will help strengthen existing peace programs and forge new programs that address all aspects of building a culture of peace. Programs will include analysis of the roots of violence, including inter-familial violence, and the issue of mutual respect between genders; and support training in non-violent conflict resolution at all levels.

9.7 Will seek an international court of justice on environmental crimes during times of conflict.

9.8 Will seek to amend the international rules of military engagement to ensure that natural resources are adequately protected in conflicts.

9.9 Will fight against the US National Missile Defence Project, and work towards the demilitarisation and denuclearisation of space.

10. Acting globally

10.0 The Global Greens are independent organisations from diverse cultures and backgrounds who share a common purpose and recognise that, to achieve it, we must act globally as well as locally.

The Greens –

10.1 Will work cooperatively to implement the Global Greens Charter by taking action together on issues of global consequence whenever needed.

10.2 Will support the development of Green parties, political movements and youth networks around the world.

10.3 Will assist, at their request, other Green parties and movements including by:

- providing observers at elections to help ensure that they are free and fair

- encouraging voters to enrol and vote Green in their home countries.

10.4 Will adopt and put into practice in our own organisations the democratic principles we seek in broader society.

10.5 Will act as a model of participatory democracy in our own internal organisation at all levels.

10.6 Will encourage cooperation between the global Green parties to ensure that member parties are consulted, educated and have equal capacity to influence global positions of the Greens.

10.7 Will encourage Green parties to show leadership in establishing policies guaranteeing transparent and decentralised structures, so that political power and opportunity is extended to all members; and in developing new political models which better meet the challenges of sustainable development and grassroots democracy.

10.8 Will avoid sources of finance that conflict with our vision and values.

10.9 Will avoid cooperation with dictatorships, sects, or criminal organisations and with their dependent organisations, particularly in matters of democracy and human rights.

10.10 Will strengthen our links with like-minded community organisations and with civil society organisations, such as those that mobilised in Seattle; we are one part, with them, of the growing consciousness that respect for the environment, for social and human rights, and for democracy, has to prevail on the economic organisation of the world.

10.11 Will support each other personally and politically with friendship, optimism and good humour, and not forget to enjoy ourselves in the process!

Acknowledgements

My thanks for help with this book go to Margaret Blakers, Louise Crossley, Helen Gee, Ian Lowe, Christine Milne, Ben Oquist and Paul Thomas; to my expert, friendly typist and, in particular, my editor Meredith Rose.

The section on Nunavut in the chapter 'Indigenous Australia' is based on an article I wrote for *The Australian* on 11 April 2000. An earlier version of the chapter on Farmhouse Creek was published in Helen Gee's book *For the Forests*, published by the Wilderness Society in 2001; an earlier version of a section of the chapter on the Australian Bush Heritage Fund was published in the July 1990 edition of *Habitat*, the magazine of the Australian Conservation Foundation.

Sources for quoted material not identified in the text are as follows: PAGE 7, Thomas Berry, *Earth and Faith: A Book of Reflection for Action* (ed. Libby Bassett, United Nations Environment Programme, 2000); PAGE 10, off-the-cuff speech by Vandana Shiva; PAGE 15, Kassar's and James's work is cited in *Green Futures*, Number 43, November/December 2003, pp. 20–22; PAGES 34–5, the letter writer is Josef Schofield; PAGE 38, Munich Re is quoted from ABC News Online, 30 December 2003; PAGE 39, Tony Coleman, 'The Impact of Climate Change on Insurance against Catastrophes' (Insurance Australia Group, undated); PAGE 42, Steffen W. et al., *Global Change and the Earth System: A Planet Under Pressure* (International Geosphere-Biosphere Programme, Springer-Verlag, New York, 2004); PAGES 45–6, Sarojini Krishnapillai, 'Climate Bullies', *Arena Magazine*, November 2002, p. 61; PAGE 49, 'Warnings from the Bush: The Impact of Climate Change on the Nature of Australia', prepared by Anna Reynolds for Climate Action Network Australia, 2002; PAGE 50, Jane Cadzow ,'The Graying of Labor', *The Age*, 14 August 1993; PAGES 53–4, David Karoly, James Risbey & Anna Reynolds, 'Global Warming Contributes to Australia's Worst Drought' (report produced by the Worldwide Fund for Nature, Sydney, 2003, pp. 134–5); PAGE 73, www.ucsusa.org; PAGES 78–9, www.wagingpeace.org; PAGE 135, Jack Kyle quoted in the *Advocate*, 24 March 1987; PAGE 145, *The Voyage of Captain Bellingshausen to the Antarctic Seas 1819–1821*, ed. Frank Debenham, Hakluyt Society, 1945; PAGES 158–9, Peter Jull, 'Negotiating Indigenous Reconciliation: Territorial Rights and Governance in Nunavut', *Arena Journal*, No. 13, 1999, pp. 17–23; PAGE 162, extract from *Story About Feeling* (Bill Neidjie, ed. Keith Taylor, Magabala, 1989) reproduced with permission from the copyright holders and Magabala Books Aboriginal Corporation, Broome; PAGES 194–5, Rick Sieman, Ron Arnold, James Watt, David Bills and Col Dorber are quoted in a paper titled 'Bombs and Bloody Noses: Dirty Tricks and Violent Harassment', given by Bob Burton at the Defending the Environment Conference in Adelaide, 21 May 1995; PAGE 207, 'End of the Road: Let's Accept that There is no Way Back for Asia's Big Cats, *Asiaweek*, 5 May 1993, pp. 35–39; PAGES 227–8, the Canadian letter writer was Will Arlow; PAGE 230, *The Manly Daily*, 24 October 2003, p. 28.

Photograph Credits

Page 1	© *The Age*
Pages 2–3	(top) Paul Smith; (bottom left) Tony Booth; (bottom right) Craig Hardy
Page 4	Ross Scott
Page 5	(top) © *The Mercury*; (bottom) Bob Brown
Page 6	(top) photographer unknown; (bottom) Rodney Braithwaite
Page 7	(top) © *The Mercury*; (bottom) Bob Brown
Pages 8–10	all photographs by Bob Brown
Page 11	both photographs by Tim Cole
Pages 12–13	all photographs by Bob Brown
Page 14	(top) Tim Cole; (bottom) © Reuters
Page 15	(top) photographer unknown; (bottom) © Fairfax
Page 16	(top) John McCallum; (bottom) Roger Lovell.

Every effort has been made to locate the copyright holders of printed and photographic material, and the publisher welcomes hearing from anyone in this regard.

Index

Abbott, Tony 224, 226, 230
Aboriginal cave stencils 123
Aboriginal people
  genocide 166–7
  relation to land 155–64
  and land rights 121, 125,
    156–61
  stolen generations 135
  Tasmanian 86–7, 166–8,
    174
Abt Wilderness Railway 33
Al Qaeda 196, 216
Allen, Woody 74
Alta River (Norway) 29
Andrew, Neil 221, 222, 224,
  225
Andromeda Creek 86
Antarctica 42, 44, 137–42,
  146–54
  mining
Antarctic Treaty 139, 140,
  147, 153
Armstrong, Lance 119
Arnold, Ron 195
Aspley River 240
Association of Consumers of
  Electricity 31

Attwater's prairie chicken
  242–3
Ausalian Bush Heritage Fund
  238–44
Australian Conservation
  Foundation 9
Australian Newsprint Mills
  87, 88

Bacon, Jim 91, 105, 133, 136
Balmford, Andrew 210
Bari, Judi 196–7, 201
Barnes, Jimmy 97
Bartholemew I 6
Bates, Gerry 118–19
bats 187–8
Bay of Fires 165–75
Bega Valley 239
Bellamy, David 28, 85
Berry, Thomas 7
Betancourt, Ingrid 191–2, 202
Bills, David 195
bird flu 63
birds
  extinction of 110–12, 143
  migrating 106–7, 110–12,
    115, 116

Black, Murray 29
Blair, Tony 65
Blakers, Margaret 55, 107, 155
Blue Tier 92
blue whales 141, 142–3
Bolkus, Nick 221
Bonyhady, Tim 188
Booth, Kim 136
Borneo 192–3
Brandis, George 228
Brazil 191
Bruny Island 92
Buddhist Gyoto monks 97
Bush, George W. 7, 8, 13, 43, 65, 214–33
Bush, George Snr 137–8, 139, 141
Bush, Laura 219, 221
bushfires 38, 48, 53, 54

Cain government 184
Calvert, Paul 225
Canada 157–8
Cape Grim 40–1, 43
carbon-dioxide
  emissions 54
  levels 40, 47
carbon tax 57
Carey, Peter 97
Carlyle, Thomas 74
Carnarvon Station Reserve 240
Cassen, Robert 68

Central Plateau 92, 122
Central Queensland Cement
  company 187–9
Chapel Tree 104
Charles Darwin Reserve 240
Chereninup 240
Cherney, Darryl 196–7
Chin Jin 218, 226
China
  paper mills 82
  security agents in Australia
    225–6
  and Tibet 216–17, 225, 227–8
  see also Hu Jintao
Chipman, Barry 97, 104
chlorofluorocarbons (CFCs) 58, 59
Choi Yul 107
Chomolungma 43
Choony, Kim 109
Chung Mong-hun 115
Clark, Helen 46
clearfelling see logging
Climate Action Network
  Australia 48
climate change, human-
  induced 37–8, 48–9
coal exports 56
coastline, Tasmanian 165–75
Coca-Cola 171
Cold War 4, 75
Coles Bay 175

Colombia 191–2
Conellan, Karen 181
Convention on the Conservation of Antarctic Marine Living Resources 142
Cook, Captain 162–3
Costanza, Robert 210, 211
Courtenay, Bryce 97
Crean, Simon 221
Crossley, Louise 147–8
Cundall, Peter 97
Currumbin Valley Reserve 240

Daintree rainforests 212, 239
Dalai Lama 7–8, 11
death 74–5
deforestation 73
democracy, global 65–6, 69
demonstrations, non-violent 18, 19, 24–5, 177–84
dengue fever 44–5
Denison River Valley 123
Denison Star 20
Dhondup Phun Tsok 218
Diesendorf, Mark 51
dingo 204
disease 44–5, 62–3
Doctors for Forests 89
Dombrovskis, Peter 28
Dorber, Col 195
Douglas-Apsley National Park 121

Downer, Alexander 213, 226
Doyle, Adrian 97
drought 38, 48, 52–4
Drys Bluff 234–6, 240
Drys Bluff Forest Reserve 236
Dunphy, Milo 9

Earth Summit 10–11, 45, 80, 81
'ecologically sustainable' harvesting of forests 52, 93, 96
economic policies, sustainable 69, 203–4, 209–13
ecosystems 66–7
ecotourism 169–70
    see also tourism
education
    free tertiary 57–8
    primary-school 123–4
Edwards, Terry 104
Ehrlich, Paul 62
Einstein, Albert 10
El Grande 89
El Niño 53
electricity generation 91
Ellis, Bob 97
energy
    consumption 54, 56–7, 91
    policy 56
    'renewable' 91
Energy Research and Development Corporation 58

Energy Resources Australia 201–2

environmental laws 71, 135, 183, 184–6

environmental loss 203–13

environmental protection 211–13

Erith Island 239

Ethabuka Station 240–1

Eucalyptus
  delegatensis 84
  globulus 91
  obliqua 84
  regnans 82–3, 84, 85

evolution 74–8

extinction 67, 77–8, 208–9
  birds 110–12
  global-warming related 49–51
  great auk 143–4,
  thylacine 204–6
  tigers 206–8

Farmhouse Creek 123, 135, 176–86, 197–200

fauna
  conservation 187–8, 241
  and global warming 49–51
  Mt Etna 187–8
  and Saemangeum tidal flats 106–16
  Styx Valley 83–4, 91, 92, 93

Field, Michael 94, 95, 118, 120, 124, 125, 126, 127, 131–4

fishing 152–3

Flanagan, Richard 97, 102

Flinders Island 166

flora
  conservation 241
  and global warming 49, 51
  Styx Valley 82–5, 87–94

Florentine Valley 89, 92

Flores, Rodolfo Montiel 191

Foot, Geoffrey 32

Forage, Mary 26

Forest Industries Association of Tasmania 104

Forest Reform Bill 127–32, 134

forests
  conservation and sustainable development 80
  'ecologically sustainable harvesting' 52, 93, 96
  as furnaces 91
  plantations 91
  Tasmanian 81–2, 87–105
  see also logging, woodchipping, rainforests, Regional Forest Agreements

Forestry Tasmania 83, 84, 88, 90, 91, 92, 94, 103, 125

Fossey, Dian 192
fossil fuels 59, 73
  consumption of 47–8
  government subsidies for 51
Fox, Vicente 191
Franklin River 17–35, 85,
  121
Freedom of Information 90,
  120–1, 125
free-trade agreement,
  Australia–US 218, 223,
  224
Frenchmans Cap 17
Freycinet National Park 122
Friendly Beaches 121, 239

Gandalf's Staff 105
Garcia, Teodoro Cabrera 191
Gay, John 94, 102
gay and lesbian law reform
  121, 125, 135
Geeveston 178
genetic engineering 11
Geneva Convention 216
ghost bat 188
Global Commons Institute 47
global governance 64–7,
  72–4, 78–9
global warming 11, 36–59,
  143, 152
  and extinction 49–51
  human-induced 52–3
  solution for 47–8, 55–9

globalisation, economic 65,
  232, 233
Goldman Environmental Prize
  137, 191, 193–4, 238
Goonderoo 240
Gordon River 17, 33, 122
Gore, Brian 218
gorillas 192
Gormley, John 14
Gray, Gary 50
Gray, Robin 18, 24, 27, 28,
  30, 36, 94, 118, 120, 123,
  124, 133, 134, 177, 236
great auk 143–4
Great Barrier Reef 49, 212
Great Western Tiers 92, 236
greed 5, 12–13, 14, 45–7,
  63–4, 79, 144, 185–6
Green, Bryan 170, 175
Green Korea United 107
greenhouse gas 39–40, 46,
  48, 54–5, 57, 59
Greenie Acres camp 19, 22,
  25
Greenpeace 105, 138, 140,
  151
Greens, the 1–4, 13, 60, 70,
  71, 74, 79, 83, 185, 203,
  214, 215, 214–33
  balance of power in
    Tasmania 117–36
  and education 1–2, 57–8,
    123–4

and the economy 79
energy policy 55–6, 57–8, 59
and human rights 71, 214–33
and humanitarianism 2, 70,
    71, 232
Griffith, Jeremy 205
Griffiths, Rachel 97
Groom, Ray 134–5, 184, 189
Guantanamo Bay 216, 217,
    218, 224
Gulf Stream 42
Gunns Pty Ltd 93–4, 103, 126

Habib, Mamdouh 216, 217,
    220, 222
    wife of 217, 220–1, 223
    son of 217, 222
habitat loss 208–13
hailstorms 38–9
Hales, Simon 44
Hamill, Denny 19
Han Suyin 217
happiness 1, 4, 15, 163–4
Hawke, Bob 28, 29, 90, 139,
    140
Hawke, Hazel 28
Hean, Brenda 184–5
heatwaves 37, 38, 39–41
Henderson, Judy 189, 190,
    240
Hicks, David 216, 217
Hildegard of Bingen 5
HIV/AIDS 63

Hollister, Di 119
Hope-Jones, Ralph 178
Houghton, John 37–8
Howard, John 7, 93, 115,
    159–60, 167, 221, 223, 228
    and global poverty 64–5
    and global warming 51–2
    and refugees 2, 46
    and Regional Forest
        Agreements 51–2, 81–2, 90
Howard government 48, 51,
    58, 116, 212
Hoysted, Phillip 177
Hu Jintao 215, 216, 217–18,
    225–8
human rights 214–33
Hunter Island 241
Huon Valley 121
Hydro-Electric Commission,
    Tasmanian 18, 20, 23–4,
    30, 31, 32
hydro-electric power 17, 23
Hydro Tasmania 125
Hyundai 106–16, 207

immigration
    Australia 69–70, 71
India 68
inequality, world 46, 48,
    63–4, 66, 78–9
    see also poverty
insurance and natural
    disasters 38

Insurance Australia Group 38
International Geophysical
  Year 139
International Geosphere-
  Biosphere Programme 42
International Labor
  Organization 63
International Whaling
  Commission 142
Irwin, Steve 228
Italy 67–8

J Lee M 19, 20, 25
Jabiluka 161, 201
James, Oliver 15
Japan
  paper mills 52, 82, 89
John Paul II 6, 12
Jones, Alan 228–9
Jones, Ross 240
Judbury 91
Julia Falls 86
Jull, Peter 158

Karoly, David 53
Kassar, Tim 15
Keating, Paul 90, 139–40
Kelly, Paul 97
Kelly, Petra 73–4
Kelly Basin 20, 122
Kemp, David 112, 115
Kenny, Steven 217
Kent, Bill 181

Ki Seop Lee 112, 115
Kilimanjaro 43
Kim Myung-ja 112
Kojonup 239
Korean Federation for
  Environmental Movement
  107, 109, 114, 116
krill 143, 152
Kyle, Jack 135
Kyoto Protocol 46, 48

Labor–Green Accord 120–34,
  236
Lake Pedder 23, 31, 184
Lamb, Robert 111
landslides 41
Latham, Mark 90
Law, Geoff 103, 128
Lawrence, Carmen 219
Laws, Zana 151
Lea, Geoffrey 30
Lea Tree 20, 30
Lemonthyme Valley 179
Lennon, Paul 102, 104, 135
Liffey Baptist Youth Camp 24
Liffey Falls Forest Reserve
  236
Liffey Valley 234–6, 240
Lightfoot, Ross 224
Little Fisher Valley 122
living standards, inequality in
  45–8, 63–4
  see also poverty

Llewellyn, David 125, 126,
     130, 135
logging 41, 80–2, 82, 87–105,
     121, 125–6, 133–4, 176–7,
     179–85, 189, 207, 235
   clearfelling 92–3, 96, 197
   effects on carbon-dioxide
     levels 52
   and taxpayers' money 93–6
   see also woodchipping
Lowe, Doug 23

McDermott, Harry 26
McKim, Nick 136
McKinney, Judith Wright 9
McLean, Hugh 179
Macquarie Harbour 17, 19,
     20, 122
Macquarie Island 144–6,
     148, 154
Maddox, Grant 151
Madrid Protocol 140, 151
malaria 63
Malley, James 205
Manser, Bruno 192–3
market fundamentalism 61,
     65, 69, 70, 73, 79, 155,
     163, 203–4, 208–9, 233
Marr, Alec 182
Mathinna 166–7
Mawson, Sir Douglas 145
Maydena Range 85, 87
Mendes, Chico 191

Menuhin, Yehudi 35
Mersey Bluff 122
Mexico 191
Meyer, Aubrey 47
Mifsud, Brett 82
Milne, Christine 119, 123–4,
     132, 135, 228
mining 139–40, 187–9
Mirrar people 201–2
Morris, Tim 136
Morrison, Reg 19–20
Mother Cummings Peak 184
Mount Tree 82
Movement for a New Society
     25
Mt Etna 187–8, 201
Mt Everest 43
Mt Kosciuszko 49
Mt William National Park 169
Muir, John 8
Murphy, Lionel 33
Murray-Darling Basin 49, 53

Naess, Arne 8–9
national parks 95, 98–100,
     121, 126, 135, 236
Native Title Amendment 156
natural disasters 38, 48
   see also storms, bushfires
natural resources 73
nature, human connection
     with 5–15, 159, 160–4,
     208–9

Nature Conservancy, the 238, 241–3
Navarro, Ricardo 10
Neidjie, Bill 161–2
Nettle, Kerry 65, 214, 217, 218, 223, 224–5
New York Stock Exchange 64
Newchurch, Michael 59
Newton-John, Olivia 97
Nichols, Nick 196
Noranda 119
Norske Skog 88
North Broken Hill 119
Nothofagus cunninghamii 85
Nunavut, self-governance 157–9
Nyularimma, Wadjularbinna 155, 156, 159

Ochoa, Digna 191
Oquist, Ben 2, 11, 219
Organ, Michael 217, 221, 225
ozone layer 58–9

Patagonian toothfish 152–3
Patmore, Peter 123, 124, 125
Pearsall, Geoff 182
Penan people 193
penguins 146, 151
Perched Lake 20
Pereira, Fernando 192

Picton Valley 123, 185, 199–200
Planter Beach 174
Planet Ark 97
political donations 90
population
    Australian 68–70
    global 7, 11, 60–3, 68, 72–3
    growth 60–3, 66–8, 72
    stabilisation 73
    zero growth 70, 71
poverty 4, 7, 11, 12–13, 62, 63, 69, 73
Powell, Colin 11
Price, Max 184
Prostanthera lamiaceae 85
Putt, Peg 135, 136, 191

Quakers 24

Rainbow Warrior 192
rainforests 49, 83, 85, 86, 212
Raven, Peter 209
recycling 56–7
Reece, Eric 31, 33, 126
refugees 2, 46, 71
Regional Forest Agreements 51–2, 81–2, 89, 90, 95
Regional Forest Agreements Act 95
Reidy, Christopher 51

Reimer, Andrew 229
Renewable Energy (Electricity)
  Act 2000 91
Resource Planning
  Development Commission
  174
Reynolds, Anna 53
Richardson, Graham 90, 122,
  185
Richter, Judy 179, 181, 183
Rio Tinto 51
Risbey, James 53
Risby, Anthony 183, 184
Risby Forest Industries 183
Robinson, George 167
Rocard, Michel 140
Rock Island Bend 28
Roh Moo-hyun 112–14, 115
Rojas, Clara 191, 192, 202
Rolley, Evan 92
Rouse, Edmund 120, 126
R.S. Graham and Associates 98
Rundle, Tony 136
Ryan, John 14

Saemangeum tidal flats
  106–16
Sagarmatha 43
Samson, Clive 145
Sanders, Norm 18, 21–2,
  183–4
Sarah Island 21
Saro-Wiwa, Ken 194

Saunders, Bernard 190
Sawyer, Steve 140–1
Schellnhuber, John 37
Schieffer Tom 229
sea levels 43, 44, 45–6
seals 144–5, 146
Sealth, Chief
Seyyed Hossein Nasr 6
Shell oil company 194
Shiva, Vandana 10
Shoalhaven River 240
Siberian tiger 207
Sieman, Rick 194–5
Simpson Desert National Park
  240
Skinner, Ian 238
Smith, Neil 184
Smith, Paul 234
South Korea
  paper mills 52, 82
  tidal flats 106–16
species loss 208–13
solar
  energy 59
  hot water 57
  power 51, 55
Sophia Peak 122
South West National Park 185
St Bonaventure 6
storms 38–9, 41, 44, 46
Strahan 26, 33
Styx Valley 52, 80–105, 126
  Aboriginal occupation 86–7

campaign to save 96–105
logging 82, 87–97
rainforests 83, 85, 86
fauna 83–5, 94–5
flora 83–4, 87–94
national park 98–100
Sun Fund Bill 55, 57

1080 poison 93, 206
Tampa 2
Tarcutta 240
Tarkine Wilderness 92, 126,
  206, 218
Tasman Peninsula 92
Tasmanian Conservation Trust
  177, 236, 239
Tasmanian Logging
  Association 190
Tasmanian politics 118–36
Tasmanian State Coastal
  Policy 172–3
Tasmanian tiger *see* thylacine
Tasmanian Wilderness Society
  17–18, 25, 32, 35, 102,
  103–4
Tasmanian Wilderness World
  Heritage Area 98, 121,
  185, 236
Taylor, Kath 162
terrorism 38, 63–4, 78–9, 93,
  216, 218, 232–3
Tsersing Deki Tshoko 218
Thailand

tourism 171–2
Thomas, Paul 136, 165
Thompson, Chris 51
Thompson, Jack 97
Thoreau, Henry David 153
thylacine 204–6, 208
Tibet 216–17, 218, 226, 227
tigers 206–8
Timber Communities
  Australia 96–7, 104
tourism 121, 122, 127
  Bay of Fires 169–72
  ecotourism 169–70
  Franklin River 33
  need to regulate 146–50
  Styx Valley 98–9
  Thailand 171–2
Truchanas Huon Pine Reserve
  123
tuberculosis 63
Tuvalu 45–6
Tyenna Valley 87
Tyndall Centre for Climate
  Change Research 37

Union of Concerned Scientists
  72–3
United Nations Framework
  Convention on Climate
  Change 44
United States
  anti-environmentalism
    194–6

at 2002 Earth Summit 11
environmental activism
   196–7
greenhouse gas 46, 48
philanthropy 238, 241–3

Valley of Giants 88, 97–8,
   102–5
Vatican 61, 67
von Bellingshausen, Fabian
   145

Walkden, Les 102
Walsh, Terence 190
Watt, James 195
wealth and society 62, 63–5
Weate, Cate 219
Werikhe, Michael 193–4
Wetlands and Birds Korea
   107
Whale Point 121
whaling 141–3
wilderness, definition of
   234–5
Wilderness Society 128
   and Farmhouse Creek 177–
      8, 180

and Franklin blockade 23,
   24, 25, 28, 32, 35
and Styx campaign 83,
   96, 97–8, 100, 101, 102,
   103–5
Wilkie, Andrew 219
Williams, Neville 159
Williams, Stephen 49
Williamson, John 97
Wise Use movement 195
Wood, Danielle 97
woodchipping 82, 88–95,
   96–7, 125–7, 135, 176–7,
   183–4, 190, 200
Woollacott, Martin 68
World Heritage
   areas 121, 126, 146, 154
   Committee 18, 122
   Convention 29
World Trade Organization
   66, 69
Worldwide Fund for Nature
   (WWF) 53
Wright, Judith see McKinney,
   Judith Wright

Zieria arborescens 85